Aliyefungwa Siri

This book is based on real conversations and interactions with real notorious criminals in a variety of settings over a span of ten years.

This book is intended as an educational volume only. The information given here is designed to help society understand what actually transpire inside the prison, and hopefully help society understand what actually transpire inside the prison, additionally help those that is at-risk make informed decisions concerning their liberty and safety.

Copyright © 2005, 2011

CONTENTS

ACKNOWLEDGMENT

My deepest appreciation is extended to all those who had the audaciousness to help make this book a reality. I especially thank those who reached deep into their souls to find the integrity to deviate from the loyalty and define compulsory rules of their gangs in order to contribute to the world and its society for the edification of Prison Secrets. I realize that you all have placed yourselves in great danger by doing so. So, trust and believe my Thank You is only a fraction of my appreciation but I Thank You all once again.

ABOUT THE AUTHOR

The Author is a prolific critic, writer of short stories. Additionally, literary work is a reflection to an image of a realization, a fragmentary of great confession to be sure but self-contained of our own nature and surroundings, but this book is far more than a novel it is an autobiography in the sense because the author was there in the very mist of the daily danger, violence in the dungeon cells and viewed and explored personally what life consist of in the criminal mind. This book goes beyond the reality portrayed on the Home Box Office series OZ.

<u>INTRODUCTION</u>

"WARNING"

Please be advised to this warning of caution: As you venture beyond this INTRODUCTION you will actually in the mental sense be entering the gates into a world that you would find shocking, compelling and breath taking that depicts the daily ritual's that is beyond the imagination of the norm.

The language in this text is uncensored, vividly descriptive and may be found to be offensive to some readers. The authors chosen not to amend any of the contents, language or revealing advents that he has experienced and been told in order to provide a reader with a raw and uncut depiction and feeling to a prisoner's realization to confine a society that goes deeper than any imagination.

This book contains unexposed "Prison Secrets"; the true facts that is told by actual participants of leadership positions in the top national known prison and street gangs. Their identity has been withheld for security purposes in order to secure their safety and family members from immediate or future retaliation of the gangs.

This book is the first of its kind that had this audaciousness to venture deep into the criminal mind and organizations of prison gang's politics and activities behind the walls. Never has it been a book composed before this one with such actual information and facts with in depth and extensive details to the kept sacred secrets of the prison gang's operation, practices, racial out looks, drug enterprise smuggling, distribution, and the places they are hidden, alcohol manufacturing, weapon's manufacturing, prison rape, and prison recipes. Everything you thought you might want to know about prison and much more awaits you within these pages.

This literary composition exposes the true life behind the wall's society call prison and prisoners call their reality.

It was a vast research for the author to find prisoners of leadership positions who wasn't reluctant to abandon their loyalty to their gang and relinquish their gang sacred secrets in order for the development of this book that is directed towards introducing and informing society about the inhuman world that exist behind the prison walls.

This conception piece of literary work has been a hostile and very dangerous study of the criminal minds behind the walls, but this book was certainly to happen, it was a must that it be composed with attentiveness and carefully detailed information which would stand as a monumental and dominating source of edification of information that is informative and explanatory to the prison life styles and events.

Fore Word

I the author decided that it was time for someone to step up to the plate and expose the cover ups and all the hidden secrets of the prison gangs and prison activities. So, I took on the task to enter the arena of demise myself in order to bring you (the reader) nothing but the truth. The actual ways how it goes down in these places known as prison, which I call the sinister beast. Those who are confined behind the walls are considered to be in the belly of the beast. This beast does partake of a pleasurable feast of gratification on a daily with human souls that become prey of the parasites that lives in its belly. It digests the remains keeping a regular bowel movement for new potential prospects to be devoured and room for new parasites to enter. The inmates are the parasites who keep this beast with a constant flow of food and surviving. I couldn't trust anyone other than myself to tackle this project without being positive that you the reader) would get the authenticity of the beast lifestyle.

The one thing that I found most difficult about composing this book was seeking the gang members from the different organizations to ask personal information about their gang functions and activities. Such acts could have gotten me killed instantly or stab by being so bold and inquisitive about things that don't concern me. It's not healthy at all for no one to be prying their nose into places that don't belong, but it was good on my behalf that I had what you would call a respectful convict relationship with the guys I approached with my request for information in order to bring this book about.

I pretty much felt someone was going to run back to their gang members and inform them what I was up to and order a hit on my life, but that never happened and it's a blessing that it hadn't. I was a damn fool to even approaching them people like I had, but you can assure that I will never venture blindly down that road again like I had to establish this book. One time for me is too many and a second time would be just plane ignorant and ignorant is what I'm not. Derange, yes, I would say so to a certain extent, years with living in the belly of the beast brings every one-off it's parasites to conform with its custom of behavior if you want to survive. What motivated me the most to get the information I needed for this book was the thought and concerns for the kids. I figured if the teens had access to information like this book about the real-life style of prison and not the glamorized fictional version of it. Just maybe it would deviate and divert them from being involved in gangs and criminal activity to avoid this inhuman lifestyle of violence, hatred, agony, un-loyalty, misery, and the invidious torturous acts of the insane. I have seen so many did come into the belly of the beast (prison) that would never see their freedom again and most of them became unsuspected prey to the condemned as a slave to cater to sexual desires or to be a flunky. There are so many vultures who lurks in the silence shadows of their own mind for such opportunity to present itself and when it does, they strike with a convincing tongue and an aggressive demeanor to devour their prey mind. To refill it with wicked and derange beliefs. Yes, it's sickening but it's a reality of the prison lifestyle, just like many other things in the realm of its world.

I am sure this book would be of great assistance to Law officials, federal, state, county and juvenile correctional facilities throughout the world. As well as legal practitioners, counselors, people who have family and friends inside the prisons, and those who are just curious about knowing the truth about the lifestyle.

Now that you have the facts, and raw and uncut truth about the prisons; you can no longer turn your head, ignores it or pretend it doesn't exist. Say it can't happen to me or I would never go to prison. Well hopefully you won't, but never say never because you never know what type of situation you might be placed in. You could be placed in a situation as I once was that landed me in prison. It was either do what I must to protect myself and family from being executed by gang members or just let them kill us all in the situation. Now what choice would you make? I did not have to ponder on such options for mine came naturally. Also please don't adopt the impression that everyone in prison is bad people or guilty of the crime they are in there for. There are a lot of innocent and good-hearted people behind the walls and every story is a different than the other. Some receive justice through the appeals court's and get out. While others may not be so fortunate and must continue up the ladder to the higher courts which could take years before they review their cases. While an innocent person has to remain suffering from the distress, pain, restlessness and injured mentally from the lack of benevolent association, hoping that he receives justice from the higher courts.

I shell now escort you through the gates and into the realms behind prison walls from my personal experience and what I've witness as a prisoner. My eyes shell be your window to walk inside the prison so you could experience what I have and see firsthand what it's like, all from the comfort and safety of your home, office, or were ever you may be drifting your eyes attentively over these deep intense strings of words. So please brace yourself as I now escort you through a prisoners' world.

Welcome to state prison the sign read that stood to the right in the middle of a small patch of green grass that was neatly manicured at the entrance of the prison compound. The sight of the prison looked like a condemned hotel right out of a horror movie. Its dull white paint was peeling from its stony brick walls.

The small narrow slits of what would be windows were bound with thick rusty bars that had been beating by many years of the seasonal weather. The tall three-layer fences with razor wire intertwine at the top, surrounding every inch of the prison concrete foundation. There rested a warning sign on the middle fence that read, "Danger this fence is electric". Guard towers rested at every corner of the prison. Between the electric fence, and the high-power assault rifle, that rested by a leather strap on the guard's shoulder. An attempt escapee wouldn't stand a chance of making it out alive. Each guard tower stood high above the prison. They looked like tree houses from a distance but without the limbs. They were shape like huts with a round slope metal roof with a rust bar railing that in circled its edges. Its Plexiglas windows were tinted dark black to keep wondering eyes from viewing inside. Two big search lights were embedded to the railing. And a red eye on top of the tower wind milled at night. The towers were not secured within the prison fences, they stood several yards on the out skirts on the edge of each corner and were high like miniature skyscrapers. They were unexposed and unthreatened by pedestrians or prisoners.

The gray goose came to a stop at the entrance gate of the prison. Two of the three officers exited the bus. One of them held a black pistol grip 12-guage shoot gun in his hand while an assault rifle rested on his right shoulder. His partner carried a black utility belt on his shoulder and a black 45 automatic in his right hand. They ambled to the guard shack and vanished from my sight moments later reappearing empty handed. The utility belts they worn were no longer in their possession. Later down the line I learn that their weapons weren't allowed pass prison gates once entering the compound.

The guards approached the bus and quickly began unlocking and opening up the bus storage compartments that held the prisoner's personal property, medical files and other unknown items. The guard shack officer immediately began inspecting the compartments. He toted a metal detector like device that had a circular shape mirror on the end of it that faced upwardly, so he could view underneath the bus to check for contraband and explosive devices.

He placed the gadget underneath the edge of the bus and swiftly made one complete inspection. After he finished, he gave a wave of the hand to his approval.

The other two officers quickly began securing the compartments. Then re-entered the bus and waited for the first gate to open. We entered and came to a halt. The gate began closing trapping the bus inside a small area. The three officers exited the bus and waved up at the distant tower. A procedure to assure the tower officer, that all three officers were safe. When they returned back inside, the second gate opened. We drove through and around to a building that sat high off the ground seven concrete steps led to its dock. It seemed to look as the building was used for loading and unloading which it was because the back door of the main kitchen was approximately fifteen feet away. Eight officers stood outside awaiting our arrival. They all wore black jump suits, leather gloves and steel toe leather boots that were laced high on their sheens.

They had matching Teflon vests and head gear with Plexiglas face shield, and thick black utility belt that hasted many different gadgets. They stood in solidarity holding a side handle PR-24 baton in their right hand and a canister of O.C. pepper spray in the other, except for one a sergeant who cradle a pistol grip 12-gauge shot gun that shoot rubble bullets.

One of the officers exited the bus and greeted the other officers with a nod, while the other two began unlocking the two cage doors that had separated us from the cock pit. The stench of stale warm urine from the bus urinal quickly engulfs the fresh air that had been blowing from the bus Air condition before the sudden stop to depart. The hard plastic two men seat had deprived me of the feelings in my legs and numbed buttocks was throbbing with a terrible feeling of soreness. The shackles on my ankles and wrists were cutting into my skin causing the areas to become tender and to swell. The belly chain that was wrapped around my waist, bolted with a small pad lock rested snug up against my upper rib cage making it difficult to breath. I sat on the bus motionless shackled to another inmate who was anticipating the departure from the bus and shackles. The rubber texture shoes which was more like a slip-on sandal plus shower shoe in one, rested uncomfortable on my numb feet. The smell of its rubbery odor was strong. The bus was full of inmates; most of them were first timers like me who didn't know what to expect once entering behind prison walls. Not a word was spoken amongst the prisoners, the silence was loud, and the racing heart beats sounded like Afrikan drums were being beating in a rhythmic tune. One of the officers made his way to the back of the bus and broke the silence. "When I call out your last name, tell me your first," He demanded with an authoritative voice. He called out each name one at a time and when he received a reply, he would glance at the picture that was attached to what looked like an index card that he held in his hand. After he finished, we were ordered off the bus and instructed to line up in a single file line. I exited the bus as quickly as I could. My legs were still asleep, and I dragged my feet because I had no feeling in them. I carefully stepped off the bus. Still shackle to another inmate who was now assisting me along the way. "What the hell are you looking at boy?" The deep voice echoed. I took a quick glance to see who the question was being directed to. I noticed an officer had stepped out of formation from his peers with his victim he had singled out. He stormed towards his mark and got two inches from his face. "Boy why were you staring at me, do you have a problem with me, and do I look like someone you know?" He shouted harshly. The young frail man didn't answer; he stood shivering like a minibike and in shock. He faced straight forward at the six feet three inch, two hundred fifty plus pound man who was dressed in combat gear. There wasn't one officer out of the eight who was under two hundred twenty-five pounds and wasn't no shorter than five feet eleven inches. It was obvious they were in good physical condition. We were directed to go inside the building. As we entered there were armies of the black suited officers waiting inside for our arrival. They all stood in a single file line ready to attack on the spur of the moment. Two of them stepped out from the formation and began unchaining us one at a time. "Once unchain step to the back wall and face it," One of them said. "You first two guys," he pointed towards the inmate's he just un-cuffed. "Grab the wall and lift your right foot up?" He then began removing the ankle shackles. Grab the wall? How were we supposed to grab the wall did he mean place our hands on the wall? I thought, I dared not correct him. They both worked swiftly in sequence removing the enslavement devices, but not quickly enough to my preference. "You first two guys turn around and strip down." He instructed. The first two inmates complied quickly liberating the royal blue paper-thin nylon fabric jump suit from their bodies. They stood nude awaiting further instructions. "Now open your mouth wide and run your fore finger around the rim of your mouth, now run your hands through your hair three times. Ok let me see your hands, lift your arms high in the air, now lift up your nut sacks, turn around and let me see the bottom of your feet starting with the right foot." He paused to catch a breath never once dropping his attentive gaze. "Now bend over and spread your butt cheeks squat and cough three times."

We were all subjected to the same body search. We stood nude with our hands behind our backs until the completion of the body searches. We faced the officers as if we were having a stand standoff. An officer pushed in a laundry cart and issued each of us a bed roll and orange jump suit. The bed roll consisted of one dark gray wool blanket, two twin dingy white sheets, and one white bath towel.

The orange two-piece jump suit had CDC (California Department Correction) prisoner written on the back of the shirt and down the leg of the pants. The jump suit top was sleeveless, and the pants had an elastic waist band and a back pocket. The uniform was made of 65% polyester and 35% cotton it was constructed for longevity I assured myself. It had accompanied a pair of white socks, boxer under shorts, and a T-shirt. We were then issued a pair of slip on jack flaps which was shoes with a ¼ inch plastic rubberize sole and a thin black textile fabric that covered the shoe. We dressed in our new prison attire. One at a time we were directed to a small office were a prison nurse sat with an open file and a pen asking medical and mental health questions that she read from a list and made notes on? After her evaluation she requested my arm to give a tuberculosis shot. I was nervous allowing the nurse to stick a needle into my arm to administer the cloudy substance that was now being injected underneath my skin. I watched with uncertainty as the small area on my arm rose from the liquid. The nurse removed the needle from my skin while gently pressing a cotton swab over the area. Then she taped it onto my skin to hold it in place. "I will come and check your arm in three days to make sure you haven't been exposed to tuberculosis," she said.

The thought of being contaminated didn't sit right with me. I tensed up at he thought. After everyone went through the same medical ritual, we were taking into another area to be photographed. One at a time we stood up with our backs against the wall holding a white eight by eleven card stock sideways directly underneath our chin. The card stock had featured my full name and prison number. That had been computer generated. An officer stood only a few feet away aiming a funny shape camera. A red beam of light protruded from it that found a target some were between the bridge of my nose and bottom lips. I hadn't realized that I had stop breathing until the flash on the camera slightly blurred my vision and then I inhaled and strongly exhaled, finding my normal breathing cycle.

After we were issued our identification card, we were escorted to a cage that resembled a pigeon coop. The square box shape compartment was enclosed with a steel screen that had been painted blue on the outside. The inside revealed its original raw rust. There were wooden benches lined around the sides with two rows of benches that sat in the middle floor, facing the cage door. In each corner of the cage you could see the big bolts that had been drilled into the concrete to keep the steel cage in place.

A huge metal fan rested high embedded against a brick wall with its rotating blades spinning at a high speed sending a cool breeze directly into the cage where I rested my back up against its surface. I probed the facial expressions of the restless, which walked around anticipating what would be demanding of them next. I was tired exhausted mentally, and physically drained by the long hours spent traveling on the bus. My eyes felt heavy. But I forced myself to remain wide awake and observant of my surroundings. An officer appeared with an inmate worker in tow carrying a big clear plastic garbage bag full of brown paper sack lunches. He unlocked the grill gate and issued them out. I quickly dug into the lunch and it seem that everyone else had followed my lead or I was following there's either way we all were now assaulting the sack to reach what it concealed inside its paper protection. I tilted my sack upside down, dumping the contents onto the wood bench. I didn't have the patience for the suspense too remove the items one at a time from the bag. I was famished and ready to devour whatever food items the sack contained. A small apple rushed out leading the pack introducing itself as the only nutritious substance in the bag. A pack of wheat bread with four individual slices followed, then a pack of meat, a pack of two sugar cookies the size of a silver dollar, and two mustard condiments laid in a pile next to me. I wasted no time undressing the items. I ate greedily with attentive eyes monitoring the inmates. Paranoia had settled in that was now directing my behavior. Moment later the same officer appears blurting out announcement to his directive orders. "Gentlemen before you step out make sure you haven't left any trash behind you. As you go out the door, I want you to make a left and line up against the wall in a single file line. There is a waste basket by the wall you can dump your trash in it, I remembered him saying and added. "No talking out in the halls gentlemen!" The cage door open, the bulls rushed through. I waited until everyone was out before exiting. There were four separate cages in the hallway lined up against the wall. Each one was singled off approximately for feet from each other. It contained one long wooden bench within its boundary and only enough room to sit. There were two single man cages that was screen with Plexiglas which was design for only standing. One at a time we were called into an office to undergo questioning by the classification sergeant. "What gang you run with, do you have any tattoos, and do you have any problems with being in general population?" I recalled him asking. Once he was through with his questioning, he handed me a piece of paper with a unit and cell number on it. I amble out the office and an officer directed me to my destination. I was greeted at the unit door by two officers. One who requested to see my prison ID, who manually logged our information on a sheet of paper that was being held in place by the spring clip of a brown clip board? The unit was deafening, the inmates was shouting across the tear socializing acting a damn fool, talking over each other. Some inmates were singing while others used their cell door as a drum.

Trash and dirty laundry littered the bottom tear. The office pointed up towards my assigned cell and my eyes followed his finger. The other officer returned my identification card, and I made my way up the flights of stairs to the third floor. The door of my assigned cell was half the size of a regular house door which reminded me of a kid playhouse door but only taller. There was a square bar window that was missing the bottom Plexiglas. One of the officers came to key the door. I had to turn sideways to step inside. The stench of backed up sewage, rust, sweat mingling in a humid room twisted my stomach and face into a knot. I flared my nose in pure disgust of the cell that had a porcelain face bowl and toilet, which was stained permanently by filth impurities that had been constantly neglected of a sanitary cleaning. The brick walls were decorated in graffiti, names of gangs and nick names of the members who occupied the room before me. Ants paraded up the back wall and out the missing back window. Cockroaches remained dormant and intimidated by my presence, as if I should be the one un-intimidated. Quiet as it's kept, I was intimidated and had every reason to be. They didn't act or look like ordinary cockroaches that I had seen. If I didn't know any better, I would have sworn they had been body building and had attitudes. I cast a momentary gaze over the floor to take inventory of the brown vermin insect gang. I spotted a few more that had gone unnoticed doing my first sweep of the cell. There were others posted in crevices and corners of the room. So, I followed my better judgment and just stepped around the ones who seem to have something to prove.

It was only obvious that the cell was constructed to house only one person, but all the different life's that it contained only made things that much more complex. Two humans and several dozen insects battling for territory just weren't happening. I later found out we had burglars, when I see a rat come up under the door that looked up at me as if I was the one invading his house. After I thought about it, I was. A slab of concrete rose several feet from the floor and six feet in length that was constructed to be a bunk that my celli occupied. There was a slab of metal same length in diameter as the concrete bunk. It was folded up against the wall secured at the middle by a thick chain. It was an additive by some inventive person who figured out a way to add another bunk into a cell that was already crowded for standing, yet alone housing two people. I unreleased the contraption of its security device, guiding the heavy metal to the floor. I noticed the white cotton pen striped twin mattress that it had been concealing. I carefully inspected the mattress for foulness before dressing it with clean linen. My celli were a first timer like myself, so he didn't say much or ask personal questions. My conversation was condensed as well. The forty-five day stays in the reception center was just the introduction to the hellish hell whole life of prison. Every day was monotonous, confined to the cell daily, no television, magazines, and board games, music, and nothing for entertainment. Just me, my celli and the unwanted insects who became my enemies the first night of my stay after sending me and my celli seeking medical attention after they wined and dined on our bodies. A hydrocortisone cream and calamine lotion became our bodies' defense mechanism at night as we rage battle against the insects during the day. I prayed a silent prayer that the prison I would be endorsed to wasn't like this reception center. My time was expired, and I had been endorsed to a maximum-security prison that catered to my sentence structure. Damn, I thought. I'm heading to the top of the latter without climbing up the steps. A place were all the killers and toughest of the tough criminal reside. I tried not to think about it, but my mind was controlling itself and that was the only topic it gave any attention.

I was transferred to another prison the bus ride was painful and three times as longer then the first. I had to undergo the same type of initial treatment I had before with the enslavement devices, nurse and being process into a new institution, but the only difference this time I had to submit to more than one photo graph. The prison required a photo that could be downloaded into a computer. So, with their hand-held digital camera they effortlessly zoomed in on my facial features and robed me of an expression that I would never be able to get back and if I could I was sure that I didn't want it. Instead of orange two-piece jump suite. I was issued a white one piece jump suit and a bed roll that contained the same type of wool blanket, white towel, pair of boxer shorts, socks, t-shirt, two blue sheets and a clear sack with a plastic cup and spoon, a 0.6 oz tube of tooth paste, a two inch tooth brush, a small comb, and a hotel size bar of soap.

After I was cleared from R&R (receiving and releasing) I was escorted to an assign yard and housing unit. I was placed in a cell by myself. A sign was placed on the outside of the door that indicated that I was on orientation and first had to go in front of a classification committee before being allowed out the cell to program with the general population.

One of the first things I noticed when I enter the cell that it was a lot bigger than the one, I recently been in. No broken window and a much better set up. I glanced around the floor for any sight of insects I sighted in relief when there wasn't any. The floor was a smooth concrete surface that seems to have been waxed and buffed. It gave off a mirror reflection off its interior. The door was a normal size that had a rectangle shape window and a tray slot that only could be keyed open form the outside. The door was controlled by the unit tower officer and had to be slid open. The cell had double bunk beds bolted against the wall right over each other, and a metal desk and stool that extended out from underneath the desk, on a metal bar that also was bolted against the wall. There were two metal shelves on the opposite wall of the bunks, and a one-piece stainless-steel sink and toilet. I listened to the drone of the air conditioner that was blowing furiously from a vent. I heard faintly the sounds of a television program in the next cell. The cell was clean and seemed to have been recently painted sandy gray. Each bunk had a thin plastic green mattress lay on its surface. Inmates approached my cell and asked what seems like a thousand and one personal questions which I only answered about five. A few offered canteen and hygiene items and the use of books and magazines but I respectfully rebuff the gesture. Every inmate that came to my cell door presented a look of urgency and a facial expression that was being weighed down by earth's gravity. I saw in their eyes the longing of a smile that had met its demise some were in the pass of their incarceration and I wonder if my own appearance would someday only offer an unsympathetic look and a demeanor to serious for relaxation. A reality I known I had to avoid falling prey to. In eight days, I was in front of a classification committee, who shuffled through files that lay on the desk. They reviewed a report that detailed my history, and recommended I take employment as a program clerk or teacher aid. The sound of employment sounded excellent and beneficial in more ways than a financial gain, until I inquired into the starting salary that would be offered. When I heard the words cents per day, I had no reason to remember the number that was administered before the words. My mind took on a blank, working for pennies was out of the question and I expressed it with an unseen exclamation point after my words. What the hell I look like working for pennies after I had paid my way through college to obtain a degree in business, just to work in some body prison. "These

People was out of there damn mind." I thought. Those who don't take up a job of some sort or attend school don't receive the full benefit of the recreation program. The program captain said probing my face for an expression as if I would change my mind. Somehow, I managed to keep a straight face that offered him no indication to the disrespect I was now feeling. The counselor mentions something about placing me on a support list before pushing several pieces of papers toward me with a gentle hand. I picked them up and swiftly glanced over them one was just a notice that the interview took place and the other was a laundry slip to receive my state issue.

I respectfully departed and made way out of the building to the laundry. I was giving the stander issue. Three white t-shirts, three boxer shorts, six pair of socks, a belt, three light blue long sleeve buttons up shirt, two sheets, one towel, two laundry bag's one for whites the other for blues, a jacket, and a pair of black and white generic all-star's sneakers.

That night same day, I received a cello who had come from another prison. He was a veteran to the prison lifestyle. He was incarcerated for many years. When He approached my cell door, he didn't wait to be asked questions. He gave answers sharply and precisely to normally asked questions of new roommates and waited for my approval to be allowed into my cell. It wasn't that he was intimidated by me the reason he just didn't barge in the room without my approval is because I might have not wanted to except a roommate and when an inmate over looks those whishes then a knife or a killing could be his punishment for his disrespect. Respect inside the prison is mandatory if you were to continue to breath. I had allowed him to move in. The veteran turned out to be a solid cat, who laced my shoes on how to make weapons out of just about anything; and he taught me the secrets of staying alive and not becoming some one's victim. He said. "Never be too quick to speak learn to listen, don't trust no one but yourself regardless of how cool you and the person are, no one is to be trusted. Never expose personal information keep a mask on so people can't figure you out. Remove all addresses from your personal letters and don't share your personal photos with any one, also don't have any one to make phone calls for you and never except nothing from no one for free, borrow or loan anyone anything, and number one rule of all, mine your own business. I don't give a damn if you see oil shooting out the ground. Mind your own business. You see it but you don't see it and if someone ever threatens your life don't take it lightly, react on it immediately regardless." He said coldly.

He didn't give me any explanation behind his advice, and I didn't ask for any either. Commonsense provided some of the answers but observing others who done all the things I was warned not to do answered the rest of my unasked questions.

It had become clear to me that the life behind the walls was cruel, merciless and a brutal place. Additionally, it had unfolded right before my eyes of the myriad of demons that was trapped in human bodies. My environment began to have an invidious effect on my way of thinking and cheerful personality. I noticed my smile had lost its elevation without warning.

I had been on the main line for two weeks and had already seen a life time of events and violent activities, homosexuals room hopping, inmates shooting dope sharing the same needle, inmates sharpen up knifes that looked more like a sword then a knife, inmates making white lighten, a crew running into a cell and savagely beating an inmate with batteries in a sock while some stomped and kicked him. I've seen hot water mix with baby oil dashed in another inmate face that immediately peeled his skin back. Each day presented another violent act to add to my collection of memories.

The captain hadn't lied about my program would be limited. I wasn't receiving much outside yard time. I was released out to the yard every other day for two and a half hours and that only depended if the institution count was cleared. The yard had no weights, only monkey bars for the inmate monkeys who wanted to swing on it pull and lower themselves on and from the look of it they were content. The basketball court remained packed with Afrikans playing prison ball. Everything goes except for groping below the waist. The hand ball courts stayed occupied with woods on one side and Northerners on the other. Southerners made their mark on the soccer field. The others played volleyball with any race who wanted to play which is usually the woods. The Muslims stood posted in a designated area they marked as their territory viewing the activity on the yard. Groups of no less then threes circled the small dirt track. It was mandatory by all races and gangs that no one should be walking or working out alone. The crips was bunched up around a concrete bench table they claimed and identified it as the gambling shack and nothing, but smoking weed, and gambling went on over there. A domino game was being played at one end, chess game in the middle and a pinochle game at the other end. A crowd crouched in a circle shooting dice. I figured since everyone else was claiming things that really didn't belong to them, I would do the same. So, I claimed the punching bag that seems to have been neglected before I befriended it.

"Yard down! Yard down!" The tower officer yelled over the yard intercom that followed a heart shocking explosion. "Everyone gets down, now!" I didn't know what to do the eruption of the gun had startled my common sense. For some reason my mind was digressing back to the signs that was posted throughout the prison that read: There would be no warning shots! Another burst of explosion roared and rumbled like thunder. "Everyone gets down! Yard is down! The warning gun officer snapped harshly again. I quickly came to my senses and dove to the damp grass then immediately examine my surroundings. The yard was in an uproar, a full riot was in progress and I mean a full riot. The Afrikans, Caucasian and Mexicans were violently striking each other in the facial and upper torso area. Those that lost their footing was rat packed and kicked violently. The inmates stabbed each other with cruel design weapons. The second response officers were called in. They were in full battle gear when they rushed into the heat of things utilizing their side handle baton and mk-9 pepper spray trying to diffuse the action. Inmates began stabbing them. Then a rapid fire of explosion erupted all around the yard, canister of tear gas burst amongst the crowds. Unknown objects whistle passes my head into the ground up lifting the earths soil before my very eyes. Inmates met the barrel of a direct blast from a block gun. Every unit tower officer was hanging out the window rapidly firing their block gun and high-power rifles. I covered my head using my hands and forearms as a shield to protect it from the projectiles that zipped through the atmosphere like falling stars. Panic suggested that I get up and make a break back to the unit. Then somewhere hidden in the darkness of my mind, ignorance advised me to just jump up and get involved in the thick of things, participate, use that knife you have on you, stab someone, anyone, a cop if you can that would really get you the utmost respect of the inmates. I grimaced at the thought. "Fuck respect, I'm not about to do no stupid shit like that, you stupid motha fuckas. I blurted out angrily at my thoughts as if we weren't the one of the same. Just be cool and stay put and toss that knife you have on you. My emotions warn me. That was a more logical suggestion I assured my emotions. Then I tossed the knife away from me. The officers had the yard under control and when the smoke cleared there was many seriously hurt and no one could receive any medical attention until the yard was secured and everyone was placed in flex cuffs and searched. Death was sure to claim some lives.

The MTA responding staff set up folded tables in front of the program offices and the officers escorted inmates a few at a time for medical evaluations. This process took hours. A group of other officers taped off the crime scene were knifing were found and inmates lay deceased or seriously injured while one officer walked around with a video camera filming every inmate. Once the yard was cleared of all involved inmates, responding staff escorted the suspected and injured inmates, lined them up against the wall of the program building and escorted them one after the other to the facility health services for further medical evaluation and decontamination from the effects of O.C. Exposure. After being attended to by the medical staff, all the suspected involved inmates were escorted and temporarily re-housed in their assigned cells without further incident. I still felt the butterfly's in the pit of my gut when I made it back to my cell. I paced the cell floor for several hours. Chow never came and the night was escaping into a different day. Two officers came to my door and told me to turn around and cuff up. I asked why. "You were seen by staff tossing a weapon on the yard during the incident," one of them said. "Damn! Man! That's all I could utter underneath my breath to myself. I thought I was in the clear when I made that move, I should have just use the motha fuckas, I told myself out of anger and frustration. I was taken to the hole, striped searched and placed in a cell in me under clothes and shower shoes. That was the only clothing allowed. Canteen was once every month and there was a limit on how much you could spin and certain items you could purchase. All food items were open in front of me and repackaged in clear zip lock bags. Toothpaste was squeezed out from its tub into a small bag; deodorant was removed from its container and bagged. I was not allowed to purchase lotion, baby oil or hair products. There was no human contact or coming out your cell for tear time. One fifteen-minute shower every 72 hours and I was hand cuffed and escorted to and from the shower. Nothing to look at but the walls around me or the wall that's right outside my door. There was no back window to look through to the outside, no way for the sun rays to shine in on you, nothing but the brick walls. There was a small window constructed into the ceiling that the officers could look down inside the cell. The room temperature stayed at an unpleasant cold sensation and its chilliness mocks my shivers. My only entertainment was the voice of other inmates on the tear and my daydreams which I indulge in for days at a time. My mind started to play tricks on me. My eyes purposely gazed at the brick wall that held my body imprisoned within its protective boundaries. My ears engaged into the steady fluent flow of sentences, that been composed with a combination of carefully selected words, depicting a story about a Las Vegas pimp named break a Hoe that my neighbor had written, basically on the lines of his own life before his incarceration. As my conscious mind concentrated on the sequence of his words spout from his mouth. I began to feel a hypnotic affect beginning its course. Slowly my mind's eye took on a tunnel vision with swirls of fog closing in from all sides. I could still hear my neighbor's spoken words, but only vaguely due to the state that my conscious level was adopting that had denied me access to the clarity of their meanings.

As my subconscious being took control, my mind's eye flashed back to a spiritual plain the revilement of my struggles of the fight from the demons within that was viewed with vivid clarity. The war to free my soul from sin was rehashed before my very eyes. It's like I was a male version of Dorothy only this was not OZ, and I hadn't never before experience such dilemma such as this until now. The first thing that hit me was like a vortex, sucking away all the oxygen out of my lungs and surroundings. I was in a cold sweat and my heart beat violently against my deflated chest in a plea for help from being suffocated by the poignant of highly toxic stench of sulfur, on a scale far surpassed a million decayed corpses. The intense burned my lungs with every inhale I attempted, causing me to wretch uncontrollably. I tried crying to God, and several times I chose. I heard myself calling out for momma over him. In the distant back round of this putrid odor was an underlying scent that my sinuses at first weren't able to decipher. Then like a de-ja vu my internal alarm warned me, that the smell was sizzling flesh being mixed with rotten and decayed corpses of the damn. The combination was enough to drive any mortal being to the point of hysteria and arousing the feeling of vomiting but being that I was in between the unconscious world and a spirit form, nothing solid came forth from my mouth. It was hard to breath due to the gaseous texture and lack of oxygen brought about by hell fires magmas that was already feeding and devouring all it came into contact with and releasing toxins that should have claimed my life but miraculously failed to do so. I tried calling any one on the tear, but no one responded. I even use racial slurs in the most disrespect way that they could be said just to get a response, but no one said anything. I screamed to see if I could hear myself, but my ears were filled with cries of the damned that intermingled with the legions of demons. The lost souls that was once confined as I screeched their miseries and their tormented wailings reached out to my soul which was already over whelmed by all the anguish my spirit was feeling. I felt that I was being drowned in a tidal wave of vibes that was so apparently clear to my ears that touched my soul deeply within, with heart wrenching sorrow and an unexplainable dreaded fear. I attempted to block it out, but even if I was deaf it would no more decrease in volume. The condemned horrific pleas for relief from the torment inflicted upon them do to their harden hearts they possessed as they dwelled on the face of the earth, living it up with sins pleasure while brushing off the lord's warnings of what consequences they would receive for not repenting. I wonder what it all had to do with me. The Satan's whispers mentally penetrated my thoughts, filling my subconscious being with his lies and deceptions of what wickedness has doomed my soul too. He replenished my sight with lust of mankind treasures in hope to break the gossamer threads of hope I possessed of regaining my freedom and holding onto my morals of the sane. Satan quickly tried to place a veil over my eyes to blind me of the joys, the love that God has destined our hearts to experience. The ever-present myriads of demons relaying satins lies about there being no escape, no turning back from the clutches of hell, and I must conform and be the best killer, predator, the top Dog of my race, lead the mass, and gain the power to make history, don't follow no rules but the ones you set. I cried out for momma again as if I was that once infant she raised into a man. The devilish selfish sinister laughter came to me in rippling waves throughout the atmosphere attacking my senses that I was now feeling more than hearing.

I heard so many voices in one and not being able to separate them individually, just all traveling in waves sending quivers through the core of my bones and drowning me with a feeling of suffocation. So, I deeply and violently gasp for breath just to choke on the poisonous gasses created from the beds of brimstone and fire while that wicked laugh expresses its enjoyment of seeing my suffering the laughter came to my ears so vividly with crystalline clarity that brought the goose bumps to my spiritual flesh. And the higher I climbed the more intensified the atmosphere throbbed with Satan's hatred that was now hitting me in shock waves, as phantoms flew throughout my body.

A steady drone sounded off that immediately brought the taunting faces to a halt, a sound of authority that I didn't understand at the time until I felt Satan's telekinesis powers being aimed at my mind, replaying the evil that I have done in my pass. The innocent people who became my victims during my hustling and all the above that constitute surviving at any means necessary. The back sliding and rejection I've had for the lord was now in the front of my thoughts. All those visions flashed through my mental, but yet still I struggled towards the exit fighting off the evil that was trying to hinder my efforts to live. I struggled at every inch feeling my body quickly dwindling in strength as Satan lashed out at me with a massive forked tongue of flames that took hold to my ankle and like a whip, wrapped itself around me with a firm grip making it impossible to gain any more ground. I kicked at this grip just to lose my footing and on my way, falling back down into his fire pit I said a serous prayer asking god for a second chance. My prayer seemed too been unheard, as I reached the bottom of Satan's domain.

I realized my prayer was heard. I had snapped back into reality noticing my body was drenched in perspiration, where my spirit had been on a journey to its demise, and that very moment I dropped to my knees and prayed in the realms of reality. My neighbors voice could be heard clearly once again as he continued to entertain the tear with his street story. I looked down at a make shift calendar I made, totaling up the days I have been locked away in a dungeon for three months and counting.

I tremor as if I had Parkinson, while taking a bird bath out of the sink. After I finished, I went to lie down on the bunk but was too afraid to close my eyes or concentrate on any area of the room for long, especially after what had just occurred. I took inventory of my personal thoughts to how I was going to free myself from this world of imprisonment but came up with no answers. The next day I went in front of a classification committee. I was found not guilty of tossing a weapon and was sent back to the main line. It's amazing how a person can appreciate all the things he takes for granted until they are taken away from him. I smiled up at the sun and shadowed the sun with my hand; its warm rays smothered the chills caressing my skin. I seduced the air inhaling its freshness slowly, holding it captured in my lungs longer than average and after my lungs became intimate with it, I released it back into the atmosphere. I even smile down at the cricket that was chirping where I stood appreciating the outdoors. I took my time going to my new assign housing unit. Nothing had change but a few new faces and a few absent ones. I was back in the swing of things. I learned new tricks of the prison trade. Like for instance, how to iron your clothes with a soap dish, and crease them with a comb, how to fold them and place them under your mattress to give it a press look. Inmates used their toilet or a five-pound paint bucket to wash their personal clothes. I watched an old timer beat down four dudes after rubbing bengay cream all over his hands first and went for their facial area.

A trick I came to learn to be useful when you are knowing that the fight will be uneven. Once the Bengay get into the eyes of your opponent the fight is basically over. You can't hit what you can't see. I was slowly becoming part of my environment. I indulged in the selling of drugs. The money was needed to purchase legal books, pay for legal assistance, typing, postage and personal necessities. I start forming a crew who I trained them in the arts (kick boxing) being that I was a profession fighter who fought for prize money in the underground though man competitions before my incarceration. Most of my crew members were eighteen to twenty-seven years old who wasn't involved with any prison gangs we functioned as a whole and was each other's comforter. Our days consisted of working out, intellectual meetings of the minds and constant educational studies. Hustling was top priority for we all had a common goal, our freedom and the finances had to bed made. Either of us had no family support. So, we became each other's family. We would sell shots of coffee which is a table scoop full for a stamp, finger of tobacco for one dollar or three stamps. A finger of tobacco is tobacco that is placed in a plastic glove and each finger of that glove is removed and tied. The one dollar is not actual paper money. It is an item of food or hygiene that's worth a dollar or more of a trade. We read and wrote letters for inmates who didn't know how to read or write etc. Although I stayed busy, prison life style was taking a dramatic toll on my entity and viewing all the things that went on inside and seeing the young kids and adults who couldn't protect them self physically from the abuse of the predators that roamed the prison compound I became disgusted, frustrated, feeble in my spirit and hopes. Mainly I endured enough of this hatred world of prison. The thought of why I was incarcerated refurbished back into my mind and I decided to create, this book to expose the game and to help the kids & teens in society to correct there criminal behaviors by giving them a look into the real life of prison and all that it has to offer any one who's sentence to prison. It is not a boot camp or like a jail. It is actually hell.

Chapter 1

DRUG ENTERPRISE, SMUGGLING AND DISTRIBUTION

Drug inside the prison are a lucrative commodity and are always in a high demand. The inmates who are in the distribution for sales and the smuggling crowd will go through any drastic measures to get the narcotics into the prisons regardless of what the circumstances they must face.

Selling drugs inside of the prison is a lot of inmates' lively hood, and their way and means to obtain life necessities and the luxuries of what prison has to offer to them. It's all about the money and having a supply of drugs to meet the demands.

In this chapter you will learn all the secrets on how drugs are smuggled into the prisons. You will learn how much they are sold for. The methods of how they are paid, types of drugs are being brought into the prisons, the way they are distributed, and all the places that the drugs are hidden. Every aspect of smuggling and distribution of drugs inside the prisons will be covered from A to Z within this chapter. There will be no stones unturned.

DRUG ENTERPRISE

Every prison gang faction deal in the smuggling and sells of drugs either to support their gang or just to indulge themselves with the substance of their likings.

On Every yard there is always one big dope man (Drug Dealer) who supply the prison hustlers who are dedicated money seekers and does not use drugs other than marijuana if that. These hustlers are normally members of gangs who dedicated in keeping a constant flow of drugs coming into the prison and nine out of ten. The yards head dope man will be an Afrikan Amerikan because many of the Afrikans do not use the hard drugs that are at a demand inside of the prisons. Additionally, they do not discriminate to who they sell to unlike the southern Mexicans. They will not sell to the Afrikans or the northern Mexican's and will not buy from them. If a southern Mexican is a drug user and his supply of drugs run out, some will sneak and buy drugs from other races without it being known to their race.

The prison hustlers are the yards small time dope men who make direct sells to the inmate population. Although they may be small time compared to the yards big dope man who normally supply them with the drugs. The hustler's profits are much larger than that of the big dope mans, but their risks are as well.

The reason for that is because the big dope man only sells his drugs in bulk quantity to the hustlers and personal acquaintance to avoid the risk of being busted. His goal is to make a quick profit without the wait and the problems. He knows the hustler's money is good because they pay up front or in advance which limits his risk, allows him to get off the product immediately and make his money behind the scene.

The hustlers are the ones who take all the risks of being told on by inmates, busted with drugs, inmates locking up in P.C. (Protective Custody) because they can't pay their debts.

DISTRIBUTION

The hustlers are the ones who distribute the drugs to the inmates. They don't sell the drugs in bulk, only in small amounts (papers & cap's).

The papers range from different prices depending on the size of the paper and the type of product that is being sold. A paper is a small quantity of a drug wrapped / sealed in plastic or placed in a paper made bundle which the inside surface is lined with clear tape. A cap is a Chap Stick cap amount of a substance that is placed in a paper bundle or sealed in clear plastic, usually marijuana.

TYPES OF DRUGS AND PRICES

The most popular drugs in prison are Heroin, methamphetamine, cocaine, crack cocaine and marijuana. The prison population has its own slang to identify each drug. The examples below, you will learn the common use prison terminology that refers to each drug.

Cocaine: baby powder, powder, white, white girl, snow.
Crack Cocaine: Candy, marble, pebble, Rock, Stone.
Heroin: Black, Black girl, Burger, smack, Tar.
Marijuana: Bud, Christmas tree, clover, greenery, mint leaf, money green, smoke, tree.
Methamphetamine: Crank, crystal, glass, go fast, hype, speed, white sinister.

STREET PRICES

The following prices are references to an ounce (oz, 28 grams) These are street prices in society and some places the prices may be cheaper or a little higher than the below quoted prices. This information is important to give you (the reader) give you (the reader) A keen understanding on how profitable drugs are inside the prisons; Cocaine $450/500, Crack Cocaine $ 450/500, Heroin $600/900, marijuana $35/40, methamphetamine $450/600.

PRISON PRICES

The prison top drug dealers only sell ounces of marijuana. He will only sell ounces, halves and quarter pieces of cocaine, crack cocaine, methamphetamine and grams of heroin to the yard hustlers (the distributors) and personal customers.

Prices of quantity:

Products	Ounce	½ oz	¼ oz	Per Gram
Cocaine	$2000	$1000	$500	NA
Crack Cocaine	$2000	$1000	$500	NA
Heroin	NA	NA	NA	$150 to $200
Marijuana	$150 to $200	NA	NA	NA
Methamphet amine	$2000	$1000	$500	NA

The hustler who sells to the prison population prices is a lot different. These quoted prices are the same throughout the prisons.

Marijuana is sold by the caps. Each Chap Stick cap sells for $1.10. Out of one ounce of marijuana you can make a minimum of 60 caps total $600 per ounce.

Crack Cocaine, from each quarter piece, which is 7 grams you can cut 15 street twenty-dollar stones. Each one of those stones is worth one hundred dollars inside the prison that is a Total $1,500 per quarter $3,000 from a half ounce, $6000 per ounce.

Heroin, a full gram sells for $150/200. A lot of the yard hustlers will not sell a full gram. But they will sell quarter grams for $100 to $125, which is a total $400 to $500 per gram. The going price for heroin is fifty-dollar papers. The heroin papers are the size of a match stick head. Sixteen $50-dollar papers can be made from one gram, which is a total $800 per gram.

Cocaine, a gram of cocaine sells for $100, and you can make six $50 papers out of a gram. Total $300. 28x100_ Total

$2,800 per ounce by grams (or) $8,400 per ounce by selling papers.

Methamphetamine, a gram of methamphetamine sells for $200 you can make six $50 papers out of a gram, that a total $300, 28x200= total $5,600 per ounce by selling grams. Or $8,400 per ounce by selling papers.

METHOD OF WAYS DRUGS ARE PURCHASED

The drugs are giving to the inmates on consignment and an agreement to the method and the time period of paying. If the inmate doesn't pay the money by the agreeable time period, the amount owed is doubled and the inmate is giving another time period to get the money to its destination. If not, then several things will happen. He would be demanded to give up everything in his cell that's worth the amount he owes, or he would become a victim of violence or both.

The drug dealer provides the inmate buyer with a name and address where he wants the money to go. Usually this address is a P.O. Box.

The buyer would have his outside correspondence to western union the money or send a money order sent directly to the address.

If the inmate chooses not to get involved or can't rely on his correspondence to send the money or meet the designated time frame, the inmate would fill out a trust with draw slip with the prison and have the money that is owed withdrawn from his prison account. The prison would send out a prison check to the party the inmate requested it to be sent to.

Then you have the prison canteen which is a fast way to pay and collect a debt. The drug dealer makes out a list of items he prefers from the store and give it to the person who owes, and that person purchase those items from the prison canteen.

A lot of times a drug dealer would expect, new postage stamps and items from a quarterly package, shoes, clothes etc. They even would accept whatever that is of value. It's all about negotiating.

The inmates who gets visits they would have their correspondence to bring them green money they would either pay the dope man then if he's out in the visiting room or smuggle the money back inside the prison and pay him then.

SMUGGLING

The visiting room is the main vehicle how drugs enter the prisons. The inmate who brings in the drugs is called "Mules." The mules prepare in advance before going out into the visiting room. He lubricates his anal with some type of lubrication, petroleum jelly, hair dressing, or whatever that's available at the time.

There are always freelancer mules out in the visiting room that's willing to assist anyone who needs his service. These free lancers are identified by their prison jacket, an informative code that the inmate population has established. The freelancer wears his jacket to the visiting room to distinguish himself from regular inmates plus it's also used as a smuggling tool. Some prisons do not allow the inmates to wear their jackets into the visiting room. However, that stops nothing and when that becomes a rule. The other sign to look for is the inmates who are not wearing a belt. This informs other inmates that they are a mule.

The inmates who smuggles in the drugs would have previously instructed his visitor on how to package the drugs, wrap it and bring it into the prison visiting room.

Drugs are packaged and wrapped in two different ways for different purposes. One way is in small size balls just big enough to swallow. Some inmates are afraid to keister or they just won't do it for whatever reason. So, they choose the swallowing method. These types of inmates who choose the swallowing method and refuse to keister are not considered mules. They don't offer their services to other inmates. They normally smuggle drugs in for themselves to use, sell or both. The inmates who choose the swallowing method prepare themselves differently than the mules do before going to visits. The swollowers would drink a few cups of water before going out to visit. Once he's in the visiting room he will continue to drink liquids usually water or fruit drinks not sodas because of the acid. The reason for this is because once he swallows the drugs, he can go right back to his cell and drink a few more cups of water and then force himself to vomit. This allows him to up chuck the drugs. The balloons float in the stomach and is easily retrieved. The inmate will have someone in the cell with him when he's extracting the drugs by vomiting just in case a balloon gets caught in his throat his friend could administer aid. If all the balloons don't come out, he would eat a can of chili beans or something heavy on the stomach to extract it through a bowl movement. There shouldn't be a problem for all the balloons coming up by up chucking them.

The way the drugs are packaged for this method is by using small size balloons. The drugs are the stuffed into a small balloon just big enough to swallow. It is tied at the end and the extra is removed. It is repackaged into another small balloon, tied and the extra flap is removed. The double wrapping is just for safety measures just in case one of them balloons break inside the stomach it would have another layer of protection.

The way that the drugs are packaged and wrapped for the mule who would be keistering them, they are compressed into a condom. The condom is tied, and the excess is removed. Then it is wrapped in black or gray electric tape and then replaced into another condom or a large balloon.

The inmates normally have a woman to bring the drugs to them because the women can hide the drugs on them without it being detected if they are asked to submit to a boy or frisk search.

The women are instructed to place the drugs in her vagina before coming into the prison for a visit. Additionally, they are instructed to wear a maxi pad just in case they are ever asked to submit to a search all she is menstruating. Once she's inside the visiting room, she will request to use the rest room. That's when she will remove the drugs from her vagina and place them in her bra underneath one of her breasts or in the front of her panties and return to the visiting room. She and the inmate would walk to the vending machine to purchase food items which usually one of those items would be microwave popcorn. The inmate would stand blocking the view of the officers with his back towards them while his visitor is purchasing items. When she goes to remove the items from the machine that's when she removes the drugs from her body and bring the food up with the drugs in her hand and then hands the drugs and the food to the inmate. They would then go to the microwave to pop the popcorn and warm other food items, if there is a small crowd of people standing in line waiting to use the micro wave the inmate would make his move keister the drugs standing up. One arm would be behind his back,

His visitor would stand facing him blocking the view of the arm, if there is no one at the micro to block him; he would cook the microwave popcorn and place the drugs inside the bag, then they both would return to their seat. If the inmate is wearing a jacket, he would slide the arm that's not facing any officer direction out the sleeve, scoot to the edge of his seat and slide his hands into his pants and keister the drugs from the front. Once the drugs are smuggled inside him, he can enjoy his visit. Now if he's not wearing a jacket there are two main moves he would make. One he would wait until count time when the inmates have to be counted and the officer's attention is focused on that or he would wait until a few people go back to the micro wave to cook food. He doesn't have to worry about the lubrication drying up because the popcorn will provide plenty.

The swollowers do not have to go through all the waits and changes once the drugs are inside the visiting room. His visitor places them in a bag of popcorn or potato chip bag and hand it to him. While the inmates eat the substance every now and then he can pop a balloon of drugs in his mouth and wash it down.

As for the inmates who have to visit behind the glass windows. The way they get their drugs is with the assistance of the inmate visiting room porter. The visitor comes in with the drugs, she buys herself some food hems from the vending machine. She eats some of the items and places the drugs in the bag or container of the empty items. She then gives the porter a signal indicating that she's ready. He makes his way around towards her picking up trash. He removes the drugs and continues cleaning.

He then requests to use the inmate's rest room. When he uses the rest room, he leaves the drugs in the rest room trash can or in the paper towel dispenser. Once the porter leaves out and returns back into the visiting room. The inmate behind the glass request to use the rest room, then he gets the drugs and keister them. The porter would go pick up his issue after visiting is over usually it would be ¼ of whatever that was brought in.

Every prison normally has a visiting room camera man who's usually an inmate. The cameraman is also the vehicle for smuggling drugs back into the prisons.

QUARTERLY PACKAGES

Some prisons allow inmates to receive quarterly care packages from their families and or correspondents. This is another vehicle used to smuggle in drugs. You will learn the items that the drugs are hidden in. These same items are where inmates hide their drugs once inside the prison. When a quarterly package is sent to an inmate that contains contraband or drugs the sender would use a fictitious name and address as the return address to avoid any connection with the package just in case the contraband is found.

FOOD ITEMS

A snicker, the wrapper is carefully opened at one end of the candy bar; by applying a steam iron to loosen its seal. The candy is removed, and the bottom layer is carefully removed. The candy is removed, and the bottom layer is carefully removed. The peanuts are removed from the top layer. Then half grams of heroin or crack cocaine is placed in the sockets. The candy bar is placed back together and repackaged and sealed.

PEANUT BUTTER

The seal is carefully removed with steam being applied. Then over half of the peanut butter is removed from the center of the jar, and drugs are packaged and packed inside, and the peanut butter is replaced. Then a piece of plastic is laid over the jar and the top are screwed back on the jar. The jar is lightly hammered against a hard surface. Then the plastic is removed. The edges of the jar are clean to give it a new look. The seal is replaced with super glue and then the top is replaced. The jar of peanut butter looks new.

Cheese Spread, Mayonnaise, and Mustard

The tops are removed from these items. Drugs are packaged in small balloons and placed inside the plastic bottles, pushed down towards the middle. The balloons that the drugs are in are the same color of the product that it's being smuggled in.

Can Foods

Drugs are sealed in cans. The prisons that allow inmates to receive can foods. This is there way of getting a huge amount at once. Can sealing machines are easily purchased. It is very easy to spot can foods that might have drugs or some other contraband inside. All you have to do is look at eh label. Normally the label would feature a generic name brand but that's not the key. The giveaway is that the label will not feature the ingredients or name and place of manufacturer.

HYGIENE ITMES

Bars of soap, usually Ivory or Jergens soap are used because they come in a paper wrapping and soaps that come in a paper wrapping the prison officials don't bother to open them because they can feel the soap through its wrapper. The soap is removed from its wrapper at one end. The soap is hollowed out at one end and filled with drugs. Then a layer is replaced to cover the hole. The bar of soap is placed back into its wrapper by the hollow end first by the hollow end first and the package is resealed with super glue.

Murray's & Sulfur Hair Dressing

These hair products are melted down. The drugs are placed in the bottom of them and placed in a refrigerator to re-harden.

Noxzema, Curly Kit, Perm Relaxer Kit

Drugs are place in the bottom of these items. The curly kit and perm kit have jars of has relaxer that the drugs are placed in.

DEODORANT

The gel deodorants hold a small number of drugs. The bottoms of them are moveable, and they snap right off. Once the bottom is removed, the gel contents will be exposed. The level that pushes the gel up through the top is rolled up exposing two deep small pockets in the bottom of the cap. Thus, us the compartments that drugs or money is neatly placed in. Then the lever is rolled back down in place and the bottom of the deodorant is replaced. There is no way that a person would be able to detect that the deodorant has been tampered with for one its see throws and two the bottom doesn't seem that it could be removed or used to hide anything in. So, it goes un-notice every time.

Institutional Staff

In every prison there is some one of employment who are smuggling in contraband or willing to for a reasonable fee. Either it's a correctional officer or a free staff who works at the prison or both. It is common to find a correctional officer or free staff member working a side business with carefully screened inmates who are trust worthy of keeping their business dealings to themselves. These officers, staff members are direct and for sure vehicles for large amounts of drugs, and contraband items, cellar phone, portable DVD players, hand held video games, bullets, pocket knives, food, shoes, porn magazine, hand cuff key etc…The smugglers are paid in advance for their services with cash money.

The inmates also target women correctional officers in assisting them in the trafficking their goal is to build an intimate relationship first and once they do that relationship becomes about strictly smuggling in contraband. The inmate would test the water by asking for items that seems harmless like gum, food, lighters. Once the officer start bringing in contraband the inmate began asking for bigger things and he would motivate her by promising or giving her a money gift. Many women correctional officers and staff members' fall for this and reed for that extra few hundred dollars on top of their pay check keep them motivated. The relationship turns from intimate to nothing but business just the way the inmate wanted from the start.

Prison gangs have particular members who are fast and slick talkers who they sick on correctional officers and staff members who seem to be easily manipulative for the very purpose of assisting their gang in drug trafficking. These inmates are giving the permission to be in the police face constantly for that very purpose.

Mail

Mail is another common way drugs and cash money are gotten into the prisons although by using the mail to smuggle in drugs it limits the amount that is gotten in greatly. Here you will learn that method of how drugs are sent into the institution via mail.

Greeting Cards

Yes, greeting cards are the transporter of drugs and money. What other way to put a mile on a prisoner's face? The correspondence purchase cards that are made out of heavy card stock, usually these types of cards have third flaps that are folded in ward and factory glued to the inside around the edges. The correspondence lays the card on a flat surface and places a bandanna or some type of thin cloth over the card. A hot iron is run over the fluid flap. The level of the iron is placed on steam and the steam loosens the glue of the card. The card flap is then opened.

There are certain ways that drugs are placed in the card. Heroin, strip of scotch placed in the card. Heroin, a strip of scotch tape is folded evenly longitudinally just enough to form a crease in the tape. It's then reopened, and the Hcroin is placed on the tape and the ape is folded over the heroin and sealed. The heroin is smashed down to even out the heroin the tape is then carefully placed around the edges of the card flap. The flap is glued back and sealed back together. If correctly done the card would appear un-tampered with. The money is sent by ironing it out to a crisp and taped flatly inside the card and the flap is resealed.

Methamphetamine

The method for smuggling in this drug through the mail is a lot simpler then heroin. You could use any type of greeting card heavy or light stock it is greeting card heavy or light stock it wouldn't matter. Why? Because there is no hiding involved, it is sent in were it could be notice only by a pair of train eyes. How? The methamphetamine is liquefied and poured onto the inside surface of the card and left to do dry by refrigerator. What happen is the drugs are on the paper. If one was to look closely at the card surface, they would notice a crystal sparkling effect almost like glitter. If the drug is not of a good quality, it would turn the card stock into a darker shade of its original color. That's why when methamphetamine is brushed, immersed or poured onto a greeting card. The correspondence selects a non-white card but one with a color tone that the mark of the drug wouldn't be noticeable.

2

Alcohol Manufacturing

Prisoner's manufacture their own alcohol on a constant basis. It's a big commodity to a financial gain. In this chapter you will learn the basics on how prisoners make alcohol. Please note: The author or publisher holds no responsibility for anyone who chooses to prepare the alcohol. The information is to inform the reader on how prison alcohol is made; not for the sole purpose of preparing and consuming.

Prison made alcohol is prepared in many ways with different types of ingredients. The following ingredients are the products that are available to the prisoners on a daily basis or easily obtained. There are two different types of alcohol prisoners make. Pruno and white lightn, Pruno is Wine and in order to make white lightn you first have to make Pruno, because lightn is created from Pruno. White lightn is the strongest alcohol you can make in prison, once it made it looks clear just like water, but has a kick like a bull. Every race has a professional wine maker, who sells the liquid by the cups. The wine maker makes his own prices on what he wants to charge, the better the wine the more you pay. The usual price ranges from $3 to $5 for a cup. White lightn is a lot more expensive and a cup of it could range from $15 to $25 dollars.

The Recipes

WINE

Before the wine is made you first need a kicker. A kicker is what gets the wine to start cooking. If the wine maker works without a kicker, he will not be able to make the wine. A kicker takes up to one week to make. Once you have a kicker you can continuously use it every time you decide to make a batch of wine. The more you use the kicker the better the wine will turn out.

Kicker

2 cup fruit cocktail with liquid
1 potato diced
2 slices of bread

Preparation: mix ingredients together and place in a jar or cup with lid. Allow it to sit. It will start fermenting. Prep Time: One week. Now you are ready to make wine.

The Wine

25 Apples
2 kool aid packages (16 oz each) or sugar
4 cup hot water (16 oz each)

How it's prepared: The apples are placed in a large plastic bag. Then mashed up, then placed inside a sock and the juice is extracted from the apples by twisting the sock. Once all the apples are extracted of their juice, the left-over shell is discarded, and the juice is then placed in another plastic bag along with the kicker, the four cups of hot water and one of the kool aids packs or sugar is added and the bag is tied. The bag is wrapped in a blanket to add heat and placed somewhere safe to start cooking. Once the wine starts cooking it would have to be burped (released of the gasses it will form) every so often because the bag will expand. The second day the other 16 oz of kool Aid or sugar is added to the bag. The sugar would cook off. How to tell when the wine is ready by taken a taste test?

 If the wine has a sweet taste then it's not through cooking, but if it's a bitter taste then it's ready. The wine is then drained throw a sheet or a shirt and the left-over contents is saved as the kicker.

White Lightn (A liquor like Cisco or Night Train known as liquid crack)

White lightn is made from the wine. (Pruno) The wine is placed in a hot pot. A small plastic bag is taped around the hot pots rim to keep any air from escaping. A small size whole is placed in the corner of the bag and it is tilted directly over a bowl or large cup. The hot pot is turned on. What happens is that the wine is cooking, and the steam is caught in the bag creating a mist. The liquid from steam will drizzle through the whole. That liquid is the Alcohol, White Lightn

3

Weapons Manufacturing

Prisons made weapons are manufactured out of just about any type of materials you could possibly imagine. Here you will lean how some of the basic prison weapons are made.

Personal Identification

The prison ID card is made into a weapon when there are no other materials available to construct one. At some prisons they issue inmates hard plastic ID's while other's issue the regular driver license type ID the laminated soft plastic one. Either of the two works. One end of the widest side is sharpened into a sharp blade. The method of how it is done it is sharpened on the smooth concrete floor. Once it has a sharpness to it rub soap on the end of it and let it dry. It would cut like a razor blade and the guards would never realize that an inmate has a weapon because all he sees is identification.

Pocket Comb

This is a very fast weapon to make and to the untrained eye it would go undetected. This weapon is used for slashing. A small pocket comb and one razor blade is all that it takes to make this weapon. The razor blade is removed from its holder and placed between two of the combs teeth to keep it in place and secured. The blade would be protruding from the comb teeth only slightly. The weapon is camouflage by placing the comb in the hair or holding it with your fingers over the end with the blade or place in their pocket.

Top Ramen Soup

I know you may be wondering how a weapon is made out of a soup. Well I will tell you. This is a weapon that is called a one hitter quitter neck shot. The Top Ramen noodle soup is cooked without breaking up the noodles leaving them long. They are cooked long enough just so they would unravel. They are laid out on the floor and then braided gently together. They are then left out until they are completely dried. Honey or table syrup is rubbed over the entire dried noodle and it is left out until it is dried.

Plastic Spoon's

Two plastic spoons are placed together and tied with a piece of string, sheet or taped at the middle and wide end. Then the ends are sharpened to a fine point

Break off's

These knives fit their name because they're designed to be broken off inside a person. They are made out of the hard-plastic tape cassette covers or hard plastic cups or plastic trays that the prisons serve the meals on. Some prisoners like designing nice looking knives so they will cut out a model of the shape of the knife they want out of a card board box. It is taped to the floor. They need fire for this process so usually they make a bong. A prison bong is toilet paper that is rolled over your hand six times or more then tucked inside out. It should resemble a cone, mountain shape. It is placed on the edge of the stainless-steel toilet seat and lit at the top. The bong would burn slowly, and it doesn't create any smoke.

Cassette Tape Covers
They use two cassette tape covers they pore some baby oil on the floor. To start the melting process, they let the cassette melt, then once its soft they scoop it onto the design model. They make the middle part of the knife thinner so once someone is stabbed with it, they can lift it up and it would break off inside them. This same process is used with the plastic cups and trays. It is also used to make regular knives and when a knife is made out of plastic and then sharpened it is more dangerous then steel.

Bone Crushers

Bone crushers are knives made out of steel. Prisoners can get steel just about anywhere in the prisons. They take the metal from a desk or bunk bed in their cell, the kitchen, the cookie sheets from the inside of a type writer, the bottom of hot pots and more. Prisoner's cut knives from the above mention items. How, you are wondering? Easily, all it takes is a pair of toenail clippers and some elbow grease and a little time. Prisoners would break the toe nail clippers in half, draw out their design of the knife on steel and use the pieces of the toe nail clipper to cut out the shape. Once it is cut out then a handle is made out of cloth etcetera, and it is sharpened on the ground or the side of the steel toilet. Steel sharpens steel.

Ice Picks

These are made from rods that are inside of typewriters, bed spring, fence, mop bucket and paint bucket handles etcetera. The tip is sharpened on concrete. A handle is made out of melted plastic tape or cloth. This weapon is one of the favorites to a lot of prisoners because once they stab someone with it, it does not leave a big bloody mess and it's easy to get rid of. Just by removing the handle and flushing the rest down the toilet. Most prisoners now prefer plastic knives over steel because they can't be detected by metal detectors which allow them to keep the weapon in their cells and on them at all times.

The Places Knives Are Hidden:

Knives are hidden on the yards around the area of were groups work out or normally hang out. The weapons are usually placed inside the ground. They are also hidden in the units and the bottom of the garbage cans. The inmate unit porters are the ones who provide this hiding place for their gang and keep watch over it to make sure no other inmates go probing inside the garbage can.

The cells are a common place weapons are kept. They are hidden inside the appliance, (television, type writers, radios), Inside the mattresses, pillows and inside the toilets. How the toilets you wondering? A shoe string or some type of string is tied on the knife. The other end is tied to a palm comb or a small comb. The knife is placed inside the drain of the toilet and the comb is bent inwardly and inserted into the hole so it would fit snuggly against its walls of the hole. This gives the illusion that nothing is inside the toilet and it will go unnoticed by untrained eyes who don't know what they are looking for. There are other ways weapons are manufactured and places they are hidden. Here in this book I only provided you with the major information to the basics and the norm to the hiding spots that cover all prisons.

4

PRISON RAPE

Prison rapes does not happen as often as people thinks and it's not how the movies portray it to be. Please don't let me mislead you, rape is a prisoner's reality and it does occur in different sensitive circumstances.

Booty Bandit's

Inmates who are into homosexual activities and lurks for new victims to have sex with, they are identified as booty bandits. These are the ones who lurk in silent shadows for the first timers and the young teenagers who comes into the prisons. The ones, who are easily intimidated, persuaded influence, weak, friendly or have feminine ways.

These booty bandits allure their victims in with kindness, friendship, protection and a false illusion of caring. The booty bandit would start illusion of caring. The booty bandit would start offering gifts or the use of his property. Such as TV, Radio, books, clothes, food, Huygens, drugs etcetera. Once his victim began excepting gifts from the booty bandits, he becomes in dept with him. The booty bandit would normally try to get his victim moved into his cell, so he could have the full range of dominating his prey mentally and physically without any interruptions. When gifts start being accepted, then that's when the booty bandit will show his true face from behind the deceitful mask he displays. He would start closing in on his prey with indirect statements about sex and sex playing he becomes touchy, feely in a playful manner. All he's doing is testing the water to see how his victim is going to respond to his acts. If his victim doesn't react then he knows he can make his move, but if his victim shows aggression then he knows his approach would now have to be aggressive and that's when. The words "you owe me", comes into the picture. His victim would be lured into a cell from viewing eyes and then spring his sexual request on his victim. If the victim refuses, then that's when the booty bandit tells him he owes him and wants to be paid with the same exact items he gave him. There's no possible way that the victim would be able to pay him with the exact items, may be similar one's but not the "exact," The booty bandit knows that, which is his whole reason for requesting the exact items. This becomes the booty bandit's foundation to stand on as the excuse to do anything he decides to do to his victim by physical force. The booty bandit would become violent and threaten to kill his victim if he can't get his exact items. The victim would then usually submit to his requested sex act out of fear for his life or he would stand his ground, and that when the booty bandit will make his moves to try an take it and if he can't then he would end up stabbing his victim, not over the gift he gave his victim, but out of anger that his plan didn't work. Normally other prisoners do not get involved or question the booty bandit about him trying to sexually assault his victim because the booty bandit going to use the excuse that his victim owes him. Then you have those booty bandits that would just knock you out and rape you without being bothered with all the pampering and delicate manipulation of luring his victim in.

GANG RAPE

Guard rape is very seldom heard of. This is something the movies would portray to the public, but in prisons you don't hear much about gang rapes. There might be a situation where several prisoners indulge into sexual acts with a homosexual or a prisoner who agreed to have sex with them for drugs or to clear up a dept etcetera, then once the act is over the person might have felt disrespected or didn't get what he was promised or agreed upon. So, then he runs to the police and hollers he was gang raped. But other than that, it is very unlikely that you would hear about an inmate being gang raped. It just doesn't go down like the movies portray it.

RAPE

It happens inside the prisons normally with weak cell mates and cell mates who indulge in a lot of drugs (methamphetamine or cocaine). Prisoners who are rape victims usually don't tell anyone about it. It remains a secret with them to avoid the embarrassment and being humiliated and victimize by other prisoners, this activity normally occurs within the white race.

5

PRISON RECIPES

The following recipes are the favorites of the prison population, which are prepared on a constant basis by those who have the means to do so. You will learn the ingredients, measurements and the procedures that is required to preparing the following prison dishes better known as (spreads). You will also learn the techniques to how they make candy, granola bars, and prison cheese. "Please note: The author or publisher holds no" responsibility for those who choose to venture in preparing any of these recipes. The author's sole purpose was to provide information for the reader's edification not for preparing and consuming.

Some of the ingredients you will read about in the recipes are obtain from the daily meals and sack lunches that is provided by the prison. The items change daily that is contained inside the lunches, but mainly it consists of the following items (1 fruit apple or oranges, 1 pack of bread that contains four individual slices, 1 pack of meat with two thin slices either bologna, salami or mystery meat. Mystery meat is a mystery because some of the meats have thin slices of jalapeños embedded into them. Some come with two different shades of color light pinkish on one half of a side and it fades into a darker color that resembles a bruise.

The other type comes in a dark reddish color with black speckles of spices.

Some days other than getting meat there would be a substitute of a 2-ounce pack of peanut butter and a 1-ounce pack of jelly, 1-cookie, and 1 oz bag of seeds, nuts, gram crackers or dried fruits. 1 pack of instant kool aid that makes one cup, 1 ¾ oz bag of chips or pretzels, mustard, mayonnaise, relish chips or pretzels, mustard, mayonnaise, relish condiments. The other items we purchased from the prison canteen and the items that's not made available for purchase out of the canteen are stolen from the prison kitchen.

SPREADS

Poor Man's Spread

This meal is identified as a poor man's spread because of the limited items it takes to make. Majority of the inmates prepare it or a similar one in likeness, but the contents are the same except for someone might add or subtract a content that's not to their inquired taste.

Prep time: 5 minutes   1 package Top Ramen soup

Servings: 1   1 mustard pack

Preparation:

Cook the noodles until they begin to soften drain the excess water. Add the seasoning pack and remaining ingredients mix it up and it's ready to eat.

Prison Spread

This meal is called the prison spread for a reason. It's the top spread of all spreads exceptional to the gumbo spread. Inmates indulge themselves in preparing and consuming this meal regularly.

Prep time: 10 minutes

Servings 2 hungry people

3 packages Top Ramen soup (your choice of flavor)

1 summer sausage (8 oz) diced

4 oz Instant refried beans

3 tbsp jalapeno cheese spread

1 tablespoon of mayonnaise

1 bag of 5 oz hot 8 spicy pork skins

1 bag (3.25 oz) chili cheese Fritos.

Preparation: Bring water to a boil and add the noodles, summer sausage and refried beans together. Cook until the noodles begin to soften. Drain most of the remaining water add all ingredients into a durable plastic bag, mix will let it sit for two minutes until noodles soften and soak up seasoning and water.

Prison Gumbo

This spread is considered a delicacy for it is prepared on special occasions. The reason why is that is because it is a very expensive meal to prepare and an inmate could eat for two months for what it cost to make the meal.

Prep time: 30 minuets

8 seasoning packs from a beef flavor Top Ramen soup

1 box of Minute Rice (14 oz)

1 cup whole Kernel of Corn

3 Summer Sausages (8 oz each)

Sliced 1/8 inch thick

1 bag Teriyaki beef Jerk (4 oz shredded)

2 Pouches of Chicken (3.25 oz each)

2 Pouches of oysters (3.25 oz each)

1 Package of Squid (4 0z)

2 Pouches Crabmeat (3.25 oz)

2 cup Okra Pods diced

How it's prepared:

Bring the water to a boil add the okra, corn, seasoning pack, squid, chicken, crab meat, summer sausage into the hot pot let it cook for 20 minutes, stirring occasionally as it simmers. Then add shrimp beef jerky and oysters. Let it simmer for 5 minutes. Cook the rice separately.

Candy

There are several different flavors that could be made with the replacement of the flavored ingredients.

Prep time: 36 hours

1 grape jelly 12 oz or your flavor choice

1 package of grape Kool Aid 2 oz

How it is prepared:

Squeeze the jelly into a small plastic bag. Add half the pack of Kool Aid and mix the two by using the outside of the bag continue to add Kool Aid until the jelly starts to form into thick dough. Then shape the contents into your required shape and. lay them out on a new piece of plastic big in the open until they harden.

Granola Bar

This is a tasty snack and a good commodity for the hustlers to sale to their individual race. The races have rules not to purchase open food items from other races. The granola bars are normally sold two for one dollar and they are made with different ingredients. The following recipe is for a basic granola bar.

3 cups Kellogg's complete wheat bran flakes cereal

2 packs Peanut butter 2 oz each

3 packs table syrup ½ oz each

3 packs mix dried fruit 1 oz each diced

3 packs almonds 10 oz each

3 packs roasted peanuts 1 oz each

8-gram crackers

Prep Time: 24 hours

Servings: 3

How it's prepared:

Put the cereal and gram crackers into a plastic bag and crush it up into small pieces. Add the remaining ingredients and mix together. Then start forming your bars in your preferred shape and size. Then set them on a plate to harden.

PRISON CHEESE

Prison cheese is easy to make and taste like cream cheese. It is a long process to prepare but what is time to a prisoner? Cheese is usually made when an inmate is in confinement for discipline reasons. In preparing the cheese the smell can be over whelming to a sensitive nose.

Prep time: One week

Servings: 2

1 milk ½ pint

1 seasoning pack from a chili top Ramen soup

How it's prepared:

Place the milk in a place where it won't be disturbed. Do not open it or shake it up. Let it sit for six days. Then open it and drain the water from the carton carefully. Then sprinkle half the chili seasoning over the cheese let it sit for a few hours and drain the excess water off again. Place the cheese on a piece of plastic and sprinkle some more seasoning over it. Then let it sit out until the next day.

6

MUSLIM

"I thank you for taking the time to sit and do this interview with me; can you give me a little history about what is a Muslim and their beliefs? I said.

First allow me to say "Assalamu alaikum"; I would like to begin this interview by opening up with the Al-Fatiha. In the name of Allah, most gracious, most merciful Praise be to Allah, the cherisher and sustainer of the worlds; most gracious, most merciful; master of the Day of Judgment. You do we worship, and your aid do we seek. Show us the straight way, the way of those on whom you have bestowed your grace, those whose is not wrath, and who do not go astray.

A Muslim is a believer of one God who is (Allah). Muslin, male and female is obliged to offer the Lqamat-as-Salat; which means in Arabic language the performance of Salat (Prayers) is done regularly five times a day at the specified times the same way that the last prophet, Muhammad used to offer them, standing bowing, prostrating, and sitting facing Mecca. In order for a person to become a Muslim he must first take his Shahabad (confession of a Muslim). They must make an open confession by mouth and with their heart by quoting the follow (La ilaha illallah, Muhammad-ur-rasul-Allah) which means, "There is no God, but Allah and Muhammad are his messenger."

A Muslim must follow the five principles of Islam which are. 1. To testify that there is no God, but Allah and Muhammad are his messenger. 2. To perform (lqamat-as-salat) the five compulsory congregational prayers. 3. To pay (zakat) a yearly fixed portion for the benefit of the poor in the Muslim community. 4. To perform (Hajj) Pilgrimage to makkah. 5. To observe (saum) fasting during the month of Ramadan every year, the holy month and must believe in the six articles of faith. (1) Allah, (2) His Angels, (3), His messengers, (4) His revealed books, (5) The day of resurrection, (6) the divine preordainments that Allah has ordained (Al-Qador).

We follow the (sunnah) legal ways, orders, acts of worship of Allah's messenger and the last of all his prophets Muhammad (Subhanahu wa-ta-ala). The noble Quaran is the book that was revealed to Prophet Muhammad of the laws decreed for mankind. The prophet was born 570 after Death and returned back to Allah (subhanahu-wa-ta-ala) in 632 after death. The Noble Quran has 114 (suras) chapters 6,236 (Ayats) verses of revelations, and approximately 77,934 words, but is said that if Allah was to reveal everything, he wanted us to know that two seas of ink wouldn't be enough for his words. The greatest Surah in the Quran is the Al-Fatihah (the opening) the one I recited before we began this interview. It's mandatory that we recite it in our prayers, or our prayers are no good.

Are the Muslims inside the prisons a Gang?" I asked. Subhan Allah, we are a gang for Allah the most gracious, most merciful of the worlds. We are the biggest fraction in the prison systems, but we are not part of (Shatan) the Devil human creations. We don't involve our self's in (Haram) unlawful and forbidden acts of our religion, Al-Islam. Islam means, peace. We as Muslim's must strive in the ways of Islam and not sinful ways of the world. The prisons do try to label Muslims as a prison gang do to some new Muslims who back slide, losing focus of their (Deem) religion and fall prey back to their human ways and functions they were in involved in before they came to Islam. We must understand people always look for fault in what's good consciously or unconsciously. The administration of these institutions is one of those who do. Most Muslims who come to Islam in the prisons are ex-gang members who normally still have ties with their ex-gang. It is difficult for a person to cut all ties with the people they are familiar with, comfortable of being around and who has long history together. It's also difficult for a person to up and stop bad habits all at once. Change only comes with time, patience, consistency with the desire to do so.

"Are all Muslims in prison Afrikan Amerikan?" I asked majority yes, but not all. There is a mixture of races exceptional of white. Not that whites are not welcome to Islam, but from the 40 years I've been in and out of prisons and I have done time in eight different states not once have I seen a white Muslim. I'm not claiming that there isn't any, I just don't know of any in the prisons.

"Do the Muslims get into prison riots?" I asked we prefer not to but there are occasions when we must involve ourselves. Especially when a different race takes fight on anything that's Afrikan Amerikan. Other races don't see Muslims they see a dark shade and that's who they attack. When their race decides there going to war with a particular race then that race is the enemy. There had been attacks on Muslims mistakenly that way and we are not excepting those types of mistakes. We held jihad right on the spot against the race who assaulted our Muslim brother. Let's not forget that there are Muslims who are pro black and militant who is the Nation of Islam. Those are our Muslim brothers but one thing for sure if there is a threat or attack on the black race, they will involve themselves in the battle and that pulls the other Muslims in. It also causes problems amongst the community because some Muslims feel that all Muslims should be neutral when it comes to anything that has nothing to do with a Muslim, an see that is where black Muslims are put in a catch twenty-two. For one thing if a Muslim does decide he is not goings to get involved with a race riot, but then he is attacked and stabbed or let's just say killed, that makes it a Muslim community issue which we will have to face. The Quran tells us not to turn our backs on another Muslim but to fight to death on his side and that is how I move, and I move with my race being that if they see Muslim getting attacked you can believe the black going to assist that Muslim; and like I said earlier you have a lot of Muslims who are ex-gang members but still have love from that gang and when that ex-gang member gets involved into something his ex-gang going to assist. That is just how it goes. On different prison yards the Muslim community may function differently than other places. It all depends on the yard (Imam) the Muslims caliph head person who is also the one who leads us in the (Salat) prayer doing services, and the (khalifah) Muslims leadership. They are the ones who set the rules for Muslims on the yard. I have seen when Muslims try to run a program that is in conducive or not in agreement with the nation of Islam. They will branch off and be two separate communities.

"When other Muslims come into the prison system how are they treated?" I asked. All our Muslim brothers are treated with the up most respect and greeted with the Muslim blessings of Assalamu alaikum. We furnished them with the necessities and provide a television or radio for entertainment. The Muslim personal library is always open to them to check out books or tapes. We have a designated Muslim who is our librarian. "What about those who are not Muslims can they come to the services?" Yes and no, we invite guesses to attend the services, but on the high security yards we only allow Muslims to attend do to safety reasons. We do try to bring others to Islam especially the teen's that comes into the prisons. If we can get a hold to them before the gangs does and corrupt their minds then we do, but most of the time when a youth comes in, he's normally already part of a street gang and has home boys on the yard and that's the crowd who he ends up functioning with.

"Are there any gay's in the Muslim community?" I asked. Subhan Allah, we do not allow homosexuals in Islam, that is a blasphemy to Allah and a big disrespect to Islam period and all the Muslims. We do not believe in homosexuality I am surprise you would even ask such a disrespectful question. We do speak to the gays on the yard and give them respect but coming to Islam is out of the question it is just not going to happen.

"How do Muslims make money on the yards?" I asked.

"We sell body and Incense oils to the population. Four to five dollars for a quarter once, six to eight for a half, and ten to twelve for a full ounce but that's the prices for the incense oils. The body oils are more expensive it's double those prices. We also have talent's that we capitalize from We Muslims that's artists who draw cards for special occasions, and portraits. We have paralegals that assist prisoners with legal matters, professional typist who type up documents, letters, legal briefs, business consultants who help prisoner's families with outside businesses, electricians who fix appliances etc. There is always someone amongst us who has a special skill in some area. "How about the drugs, does Muslims sell drugs?" I asked.

"Yes, there are Muslims who sell drugs and smuggle them into the prison. These Muslims who do this act do it on the under not in the light so other Muslims can see. They sell drugs for personal gains not for the community and when this Muslim gets caught in the act he is brought up on charges and we will excommunicate him. But two Muslims have to witness the fact that the Muslim is involved in wrong doing that's against Islamic law. When a Muslim is excommunicated from the community, the other Muslims are not allowed to socialize or acknowledge his presence while he's excommunicated. This is a form of punishment. Drugs inside the prison are a big business bigger then on the streets. And there is almost much money to be made and drugs allow a person to accumulate every luxury that is offered inside. It also gives a person power and a voice that would be heard. The drug addicts from the different races is not going to want their drug connection to be busted or placed in any position that would hinder him from being able to supply the drugs. So, they will stand up for him against their race. Then you have the sidekicks, his runners, flunkies, protection crew, business associates who he looks out for. Who provide them with the means to put food in their mouths and Hygiene's to stay clean and smelling good? Who make it possible for them to have some of the prison luxuries? These individuals will protect the one who's supporting them at any cost, to avoid any possible destruction of their bread and meat.

A lot of these guys who sells the drugs on the yard support their families in society take care of their girls; provide the money for them to visit. So, when you are dealing drugs and it's on a big scale, not only are you making a lot of money, but you are the door way for others to make money as well and a lot of inmates don't have no other means to obtain any finances to support themselves other than selling drugs. So, when a person or group tries to bring down the man, there would be a physical violent problem. So, the Muslims who do have their hands in the drug business, as long as they are not openly out with it so other Muslims can see what they are doing, then there shouldn't and won't be a problem simply as that.

We know that many of the Muslims in prisons yet to give up all their old habits and Allah sees everything they do and is patient, and knows that the flesh is weak, and the soul is easily manipulated.

"Being that Muslims are not a gang what gives you the authority to speak for Muslims?" I asked.

It's just like a kafir (disbelieve) to ask such a question. For one Muslims have only one leader and that is Allah. I represent for Allah. I am a kalinafah who is respected throughout the prisons in many different states. My actions, deeds and sacrifices for the Muslim communities give me the honor to address your questions directed towards Muslims. And on this yard, I am the only who's in the position to do so.

"Do the Muslims have a mandatory workout program?" I asked.

Of course, we have a mandatory work out program. We believe in keeping the mind, body and soul in the best of shape possible. Our workouts do not consist of only physical workouts. We have mental and spiritual work outs as well. We keep the mental strong, swift, alert and active by academic studies, acquiring as much knowledge as possible while learning to speak different languages. Our spiritual studies are from the Holy Quran in order to become oneness with Allah. The physical workouts consist of calisthenics, road work, and self-defense training is conducted secretly. The Muslim community has a wide range of professional martial artist it all about each one teaches one.

"How do Muslims feel about the police?" I asked.

"I am not able to answer that question for the entire community, for everyone has their own personal outlook and opinions about the police. As Muslim we are obligated to be at our best in caricature dress, manner, neatness and attitude. We are obligated to be righteous and respectful and to refrain from back biting, frivolous conversation and negative behavior. So, in order to do that one must not adapt to harvesting ill feelings towards no one. The police have a job to do they are under obligations to a duty just like Muslims, gang members are to their group. Once a person understands that then he would be able to deal with negative feelings towards a person or class of people. I view it this way, police must do what they have to, and we must do the same. It's all even and fair. My feelings towards the police is the same as it is towards everyone else, humble."

"I always thought all Muslims were militant and hostile." I said.

See that were lack of knowledge hinders you. If a person range of information is short, then how does he expect to grasp the understanding of things that is right before his eye's and understand it? I can't never stress the fact enough that knowledge is power, more powerful the money. Education is the key for that knowledge. Muslims are taught discipline, humbleness and to take the middle course to problems. We are hostile only in the eyes of the wicked the real evil doers. The devil doesn't like to be stood up to and challenged and fought back with the same type of aggression attacks as he uses. We are instructed by Allah to fight to death hold jihad. We are the Ghazi of Allah. If our lives are being threatened then we will do whatever we must to protect Muslims regardless, Allahu-Akbar, Allahu-Akbar, Allahu Akbar. God is most great.

"How do Muslims feel about other men raping other men?" I asked.

How do we suppose to feel? Muslims are conditioned to stay clear of such impure, wicked thoughts. Although rapes happen inside the prisons, we are not super heroes, we don't know when it's going to happen, and we can't be there to save those who's about to become sexual assault victims. It doesn't sit well with us in no form or fashion. If we observe something like that about to go down, we will intervene and stop it no matter what race it is. We are highly respected by all races and gangs on the yards. There is a for sure understanding if you do something to a Muslim, get prepared for a war. If the problem could be worked out verbally then that's the course we will take and except, but if not. We will not poke you a few times with a knife. We are coming with every attention to put you six feet deep regardless if the officers are watching or not business is going to be taking care of accordingly, and if the officers get in the way.

They will just become one of our victims also. In these prisons a Muslim does not ever have to worry about someone trying to rape him. If anyone ever bold to cross that line, we will take his life. There will be no escape, no running to We Prison Cops always have Ghazis ready to go to Prison Cops to take care of Muslim business. In the prison we run a tight program. We try to keep to Muslim business only unless a matter pop's up that effects the entire population then we will investigate. This prison life is a very inhuman place to be. There's nothing here but a lot of sadness, misery, hatred, violent and a monotonous rotation of frustration, deception and distress, and death for those who lose hope and become a slave to the life style. I see inmates on a daily basis chasing dope or the drink, anything to stay intoxicated to escape this place. That's one of the reasons why drugs are at such a high demand and inmates would pay just about any price, especially a heroin addict hell would sell his soul if he could. This is hell on earth because I see the devil and his demons every day that I awake.

7

NAZI LOW RIDERS
N. L. R.

"What are Nazi Low Riders?" I asked.

Nazi Low Riders are not necessarily white boys. We are a mixture! We are part white, part Mexican, part Asian and part Indian. What we are supposed to be are individuals whose heart is white, down for the white race. We are the cream of the crop with gangster like mentalities. What we started off as, was hard core white boys with hearts of a lion, a Cholo likeness in dress, and Gangster Nazis to be precise.

"Tell me when the NLR began and how the name came about?" I asked

In the late 70's we got started up in the Northern Youth Authorities "Preston" How we became was by twelve white boys with the folio criteria, who use to ride with the surenos when it would jump with the northerners. A South Sider started calling us the Nazi Low Rider's. It was just a nick name meant in good humor but became a night mare for many. "What do the NLR stand for?" I inquired. We represent white power. For many National Socialism but in reality, we are just a bunch of vipers waiting to unleash our poisonous venom into the main stream prison life. To wreak havoc and instill fear amongst those who are beneath us. Who are beneath us? Anyone not behind the vicious number "44" our numbers were kept to a selective few only the strongest. We were the knights in shining armor amongst our own race Captain save a wood!

Then in the mid 90's we were given the green light by our forefathers (The Brand) Aryan Brother Hood. To graduate from youth Authority to the state pen under the stipulation that we were to be their arms and legs. Their Torpedoes we were to be their training ground. Once we climbed the ladder our next step or phase was to graduate once again and become one of them Aryan Brother. But being our numbers were so few we began a top-level massive recruitment.

Our first and must costly mistake, was when one skin head became envious because a lot of them had joined our numbers causing their comrades to strongly dislike us, additionally, we took down any one in our path. Anyone not submitting to our reign they had to bow down and kiss my ring or pay the penalty. Our mentalities are so wicket we did not hesitate to break all resistance. What started as a mighty force for building our race became a modern-day S. S Gestapo force that wrecked many a good white man. We got too big to fast with no chain of command for guidelines.

In having this dominant way of thinking we alienate our own races and caused separatism amongst a race that's strength was not up to par with another race. Weakening our fold and not strengthening; although the skins and the woods never had the courage to step up and check our momentum their dislikes and hatred towards us was evident, but we still held the keys every place we were present. Every prison yard belonged to the Riders. "No Questions Asked?"

"How can a wood become a Nazi Low Rider?" I asked.

Back in you authority you got jumped in, but as we grew and became who we are today we wanted killers and not just averagely down white boys. So, you had to book (stab) your way in! Whether you are a rat, child molester, Jew or a black, blood on a knife was the way to get in. Once you got in earned your bones. You could not just get the letters N L R tattooed on you. You had to earn each letter with the shed of blood. Earn your colors or earn your letters both mean the same.

Once our unquestionable dominance was law, we began to check every person (white) who stepped on our yards. Mandatory paper work but not so thoroughly as we did in the AD-SEG's or Shu. In the lock down units, we need to see your 114 lock up order and every classification chronological as well. But out on the yards was more by way of mouth, if somebody recognized a rat, Chester. They either produced paper work or handled it but another mistake of ours was our favoritism. If a comrade fellow rider said it was so. Then we acted upon his word and putt holes. This was not good due to personal beefs, but we were riders no slipping no sliding just Nazi Low Riding 44up our gang number. The wood pile has a number 23 meaning the 23rd letter of the Alpha bet is "W" that stands for white or wood. Skin Heads have the number 88. The 8th letter of the Alphabet is "H" so 88 equal HH equal Hail Hitler. So, the Riders have the number 44 "N" is the 14th letter of the alphabet "L" is the 12th letter and "R" is the 18th letter 14 + 12+18+ 44 and 44 equals N.L.R.

The Co's in many prisons would give us the low downs on many child molesters and turned their backs as blood flowed. They knew we weren't hesitating to probe a Chester's body with holes.

"How do the N.L.R., make money inside the prison? "I asked.

"Every white man who have the courage to step foot into our domain with a "Clavo" a lump of dope has to break ours off, pay rent or give us 1/3 of their shit or get it took with a lot of hurting. If a none rider went to store and did not contribute to the rider's "kitty", a collection given to the riders care to portion out to whites who did not get store. He got dealt with severely, usually its 20% that is recommended to be contributed. But most riders raped the kitty and dared to be questioned on it. The funniest part of it all is for the most part, there are no set rules exceptional of one, Riders are right depending on what institute you are at and who's running the show and what riders are there. For the most part it was all about the riders coming up at everyone else's peril. We are plotters and planners. We plot against and brave enough to go against the grain. We set into motion it was all about do everything for the riders and don't ever go against it. "What is it like to a shot caller for the N.L.R.?" I asked.

"Holding the keys for the ride is like walking into a snake pit. You have to be on your toes and stay a head of the snakes. It is more deadly and hazardous to my health then going to war with another race. No matter how strong or how much of the game you know eventually you are going to get holes put in you. If not, you definitely are not a strong individual and are doing something wrong. That's the sickness of it all. That's why we are sick ass Nazis. We have a thirst for violence just like a pit bull. That first taste of blood is all it takes for the demons to take over and I'm a lot worse than most. See as the shot caller you have envious eyes on you with a hunger for your shoes. It's called the balance of power. One minute you hold the power the next you're leaking from newly acquired holes. Some last longer than others, but it's inevitable that you meet your demise sooner or later mine just hasn't come yet, but the rush, the thrill of having so much ruthless, hatred at your disposal and being able to put a leash on your dogs of war or unleashing them to wreak havoc and chaos with the snap of a finger is such adrenaline rush, and they are in action without a first thought, the twisted mentality of an insane mind seeking death. Staying in power knowing it's only a matter of time watching the mask being put on the falseness of their professions of love and honor and loyalty to a cause that is nonexistent. The genuine courage and strength it takes to play in this play ground for periods at a time is great.

They say you tell a man's strength by the strength of his enemies. I am here to verify the truth to that, the more enemies you have and to what level of power they hold shines ten times on you as being that much more. To face the false fronts that your enemies put up knowing its coming and their eyes are stoking you, waiting for you to slip up, patiently planning and plotting. Knowing it is going to happen but facing it as everyday life. I am not meaning to paint the picture that all comrades are all demons they are just all vipers.

"So, there are rules for the Nazi Low Riders? I asked.

The prisons labeled us a prison gang and in truth, technically we are but structurally we are far from it. The closest thing we have to structure is our churches in AD-SEG, SHU, and even mainline yards. We have meetings and vote for what actions we deemed appropriate. This action was more prominent in youth authority and in the beginning stages of our stepping into the big house. As the later stages came it was more a front, a way of pacifying the Low Riders into felling special and a part of something important, but when all is said and done. The key holder made the calls. We don't force membership on anyone contrary we pick and choose our members; some for selfish reasons, some for loneliness but we pick you, not you us and it's not for the most part, just any old body. You have to have heart or at least act like you do, but in the same since. A lot of Riders abuse the recruitment and allowed walk in, not blooded in. Not just any old wood will be elected to step up and if we choose someone, but they don't want to. That is fine, but not once have I witnessed a refusal in the 28 years that I have been riding. A lot of our ranks come from who we considered our lil brothers (skin heads). They did not like that they felt that being fellow Nazis they should be equal to us what a joke! We've gone to war and put down their lil rebellions numerous times; creating a deeper felt hatred amongst us. My personal feelings were that we were kinfolk but that was never adopted.

The history between N.L.R., and skin heads, we started off as fellow Nazis comrades, but envy on their side and power on ours drove a wedge between us. To us skins are nothing more than our servants. Peasants to serve us as we deemed fit. As for the regular woods nothing more than lames, prey for us predators. Once in a great while we find ones with admirable qualities, ones that shined above the crowd. Those ones did not remain as one of their ranks. They were snatched up, recruited into one of us. Other than that, the rest were expendable.

"Does the N.L.R. have a mandatory workout program like other gangs do?" I asked.

A few of us are into building ourselves mentally, physically and spiritually. Not the religion aspects but our soul, strong inside and out. Not so much on mainline but in the AD-SEG's and SHU's. No excuses, you did it or got regulated. The work out varied from one place to the next, but basically consisted of bur pies for strength and wind. Whoever ran the routine would say, down? The rest would go down and come up with a loud"1". We did a cadence when we came to our "4" we said "Thor God of war" as silly as it sounds being Thor was not the God of war. We just said it any ways for the rhyme and it was a mental psyche out. For the six we said "sick ass Nazi" 8's was "hating" with anywhere from five to twenty-five riders all sounding off at the same time. You can imagine the adrenaline rush and how pumped up you become.

Now let me digress back for a moment to answer your question as to how we make money in the prisons. It's not so much us making money, more like extorting money pressuring other whites. We do fairly well, if you don't freely relinquish what we request. You get hurt with the loss of it all. Most are smart enough to ask us what we need without us approaching them.

"What does the lighten bolt tattoo mean?" I asked.

The double lightning bolt preferable on the inside of our bicep usually meant you stabbed a nigger. It used to be honored but with the way prisons are now. Anybody could buy a tattoo without earning or even knowing the significance of its true value. That why a lot of us do not wear the easily bought stripes. The swastika represents the same and the devaluing of its meaning has met the same downfall as the "SS bolts". Double lightning bolts come from World War II, Nazi Germanys, but again the Swastika or Swazi and bolts basically have no true meaning. They are just a commercial tattoo these days.

The cadence that was spoken about earlier our motto is "no slipping, no sliding just Nazi Low Rydin". Our song is an oldie, all my friends are low riders, but we just add Nazi before Low Riders.

As for our structure, here is a prime example of our lack of structure. We claim to be white power but yet. We have Asian/Caucasian, Mexican/Caucasian and Indian/Caucasian and we even have a pure Indian that's a N.L.R., but they claim and ride under white power. Those that are mix breeds disown the other part of their heritage and except the white side of them as they true and only heritage. So how can we be fully racial? What we are is simple. We for the most part is the definition of German. which is "Warmen". We are blood lusting convicts who thrive off of violence. If we aren't at war with some body, we get bored and start one. We claim to hate Niggers', kikes and northern Mexicans, and the Asians are border line. For the most part we do unless it suits our needs to deal with them on a mutual respect level, but you will never see us excepting any open food items or tobacco products from them, you will never catch us eating, drinking, and smoking behind them, or sitting at the same tables. That protocol, it is the way prisons un- written law has been for cons and as with those before us. We just followed suit and respect the ways of our forefathers, plus it fits into The Nazi Low Rider mentality "Hate". We hate everyone and thing not with us and even some that are. It's all an excuse to start something violent for our pleasure and excitement. That's the only way I know how to put it.

"Does the N.L.R. be into gang raping other prisoners?" I asked.

People have misconceptions about the prison life about people getting raped. For the N.L.R. that is purely fictitious and is so far from the truth when it comes to the riders, one there are so many homosexuals no body needs to rape anyone, but it happens with other groups, but not with the riders. We don't get into others business so I will not speak on that subject you are right here in prison with me and know the people to get at about that. The N.L.R. is not one of them.

"Who does the N.L.R. stay at war with?" I asked.

"We stay at war with the Niggers, but we have been to war with every single faction. Niggers, Nips, busters, sewer rats, skins, woods, brand, Mexican mafia, Northerners, Kikes are just victimized, no heart, no back bone just weak.

"Does the N.L.R. really like the Southern Mexicans?" I asked.

"Us and Southern Mexican's use to be tight but even though we role with each other once in a while just for history sake, we don't care for them we consider them bean pushing, taco bending straight hair niggers with light skin, not to be trusted a branch of the mud race.

"Do the Nazi Low Riders use drugs? I asked.

"of course, we get high some like tar, white girl, but most like white sinister. We dip and dabble in every drug. But the most favorite amongst my race is tar and white sinister better known as crystal meth.

" Is there anything that you would like to share with me that I may have over looked to ask, that you feel people in society need to know? I asked.

Yes, my deepest personal out look of a family I have dedicated 28 years of my life to what people need to know is that no matter how structured a group may seem. There is always a flip side to every story. Nazi Low Rider is an oxymoron from its name, to everything we turned out to be. To its loyalty to its members and that's 100% true and real from a warrior who is every bit a Nazi Low Rider.

8

GAY BOY GANGSTER
GBG

He, who likes to be identified as a she, sat in silence for a few minutes looking up at me. She had a cunning smirk, deliberately prolonging the interview. I had assumed he was admiring my handsomeness and being flirtatious how he bit on his bottom lips, staring with lustful eyes before he spoke with a gentle soft voice that didn't cognate with his actual gender, but it did match his alter appearance. "Well I am going to break it all down plain and simple for you about us homosexuals who loves dick. Big thick one's preferably. Everyone in the world already know what homosexuals like, to suck and get fucked, but some of us also like to give it then receiving it all the time, and yes, I am one of those ones. I am into role playing, some days I like being the top and other days the bottom I know you probably don't know what that mean since you don't indulge in such over whelming mind blowing, physical sexual pleasure's, to a deep spiral of sensation.

An unspoken intimacy of sensuality of the erotic, "Yeah you are right about that I don't know much about it, but how about you explain it to me so the readers of this book I am composing could have a clear understanding about what you mean." I replied.

"I sure will honey, the top is a person who does the fucking in his loves ass and the bottom is the one who gets fucked, which I don't think of my butt as that. I call my butt a pussy because I can work it better than any woman can, make you say things you never thought you would say." How about we move on to another subject like telling me about your gang? "I asked.

I am one of the founders of the secret society homosexual gang known as the Gay Boy Gangsters. We are not like other gangs I want to make that Clear. We are not boastful in advertising our gang name. We are not into the criminal violent activities or harming people. We are about making money and supporting each other, mentally, spiritually, physically and sexually if need be. A few friends and I started this gang so other homosexuals like our selves would have a solid foundation to a support system and protection from the gay bashers and any others who felt the need to be violent towards us. We originally started on the streets of Los Angeles California when a lot of homosexuals was hustling the down town and Holly Wood area on sunset before we start getting busted for selling drugs, prostitution, boosting, identity theft, forgery and credit card fraud and being sent to the pen. Some of my dawgs was on probation and parole from different states and was expedited to their state for parole violation.

We had never expected for GBG to migrate as it has to other states and prisons around the world. I know some of my dawgs was in prisons in different states who had recruited more members, but that is to be expected from any one of us were ever we went. We have to establish that support system were ever we go.

"How about telling me what it is like for a Gay inside the prison?" I asked

"Most of the time it's exciting because you are around so many men and get to see big cocks and tight ass cheeks. It is wonderful. But it is not always smiling and high spirits. Some prisons the inmates do not allow homosexuals to walk the yard. As soon as one of my kinds hit the yard he's rushed by his race. Let me just say this so I can make it clear for you. Please don't get the wrong impression about us because we chose to be the way that we are, that don't make us weak or pushovers. A lot of us have major chukkas and don't have a problem throwing them from the shoulders or slashing or running a long piece of steel in a mother fucker. A lot of men in the prison get us misconstrued and feel they can talk to us any old kind of way or lay hand down, but the reality of it all we are still men with dicks who would get off in that ass more than just sexually. I do not like to lose sight of my femininity, but I will in order to protect myself or one of my members. We can be aggressive and get down with the get down also. I have been there and done that many of times, drain a few souls from their bodies for playing me to close. That's why I have a life sentence right now. I hate to think about it, but I picked all that time up right here in prison when I only had a one-year parole violation from the start. Now look at me now I am doing life and do not have to get back. You know what though and I raise my right hand up to God, to what I am about to say, so helped me God or stick me dead. Most of the men in prison who talk negative about homosexuals who frown up at our sight or have some type of dislike about us for whatever it maybe they are the ones who really curious about our life styles they are over admires on the under and some of our biggest fans. I have exploited and seduced many of men who quote on quote supposed to be hetero sexual, I am not talking about the men on the streets. I am referring to the so call hard, though guys, gangsters and killers inside these prisons, who frowns up at the sight of my kind when they are in the presence of their friends but smile at us when they think the coast is clear of watchful eyes. A lot of these guys propositions us with canteen and drugs for sexual favors always talking about keep it on the down, but they are not the only ones. It is not unusual for a correction officer to make sexual advances or propositions. I have ha d my share of turning dates with a few different correctional officers who paid me handsomely for a blow job or just to suck me off. We do take full advantage of those types of tricks. We make they asses pay swell and continuously for helping to fulfill their freakish fetish. They become our mule who smuggle drugs, panties, make up, food, cellar phones and whatever else we might need or want. If they refuse to do it, which 99% of the time they don't, we will holler rape, sexual assault and the correctional officer do not want that, because a lot of them have a wife and family and they don't want be put in a position of being humiliated in front of their peers and the public eyes so they just kick out like we ask. The inmates are a little different. You can't just threaten them all like that because some don't care if you go tell or not, but if he is a part of a gang then he has to worry because they will do him in, but the problem with that the one you tell on most likely will try to kill you first before his gang get a chance to get him. So, we have to be careful how we approach situations like that we do have a way for handling inmate tricks. When one of them request for us to sneak over to their cell for sex, we charge them, we stay manipulating. I been with men who gotten sprung on the pussy who broke ties with wives because they wanted to be with me. I had some become extremely jealous and overly aggressive about me socializing with someone else. I even received marriage proposals. It is crazy how this prison life is a world, within a world where there is no limitation to the criminal imagination. It is liking some strong and weird provocative shit that's going on in these stoops. I have witness in the privacy of a cell some of the hard core, thuggish, and heartless criminals turn bitch doing our sexual acts allowing themselves to be free to the pleasures of my love making, giving me a reach around as they pump inside of my pussy doggy style. Some even requested that I fuck them in the ass. Oh yes believe it honey, this is how it goes down in prison. You ask me to give you the real for your book and I am giving it to you without pulling no punches. The women out there in the world need to know about some of these men in these prisons who are claiming to be all man and strictly on pussy. That's only until one of my kind get him behind closed doors and then he is on male pussy or sick pussy. A lot of men in prison do indulge in one way or another fucking or getting sucked up. A lot of the men feel there's nothing wrong with getting some head and I agree with them, because giving a man head gives me the opportunity to turn him out. I get full pleasure out of seeing a man fall weak over me. It's only natural and in evitable for the men's in prison to become excited, aroused and with the desire to want to fuck one of my kind. How can they not when they are confined for months and years around nothing but men and can't be with no women physically? So, when they see one of my kinds looking all good and like a woman with a nice firm round ass wide hips wearing tight jeans hair hanging long and styled, smelling sweet and speaking with a sexy voice. Of course, we going to be enticing and alluring to their sexual desires of the need to release all that built up pressure inside of them. Some of us actually have real breast like me you know. We are the best thing they going to get and for some the only thing. I have also witnessed a lot of marriages being broken up when an inmate starts indulging in the goods. I myself have destroyed plenty of marriages not intentionally. My tricks tend to fall in love with me and want a commitment, and to prove his loyalty he ends his relationship with his wife on the streets. It even gets so bad some start denying their family visits just to keep an eye on me from fooling around with anyone else.

Some of the inmates are not shy about letting it be known they are into homosexuals and you have some that would even kill another inmate over us.

"What about the drugs?" I asked.

If you are trying to ask me about us smuggling drugs or getting it inside the prison most of my kind does both. We normally try to hook up with the main drug dealer on the yards to see if he needs a mule. If he does, then he arranges for an outside contact to get approved on our visiting list. Once the approval goes through, we'll get a visit and the visitor brings the drugs to us and me keister them and take it back into the prison. "Do you get paid for this?" I asked.

"Of course, I don't do anything for free. The going rate for such a service is ¼ or 1/3 of everything that is brought in. It all depends on the agreement between you and wham ever you are working for, but most likely it would be 1/3 without any complaints or need of negotiation that's the going prices in majority or the prisons. "Are all homosexuals in the prison part of the GBG?" I inquired.

"I am afraid not, we just don't take anyone into our society. We do pick and choose in order to keep the loyalty real and the foundation strong, but we still look out for the other homosexuals from time to time. One of our main things is to keep the GBG family dealings, activities, gatherings, missions, and attention out of the public and the institutions eyes and ears.

We have been so low key for years that a lot of inmates themselves knew nothing about the GBG's only but a chosen few who had major business dealings with us. "Are the members of your gang one race or is it a mixture." I Asked.

"We are a gang that represents homosexuals, and we don't play that racial shit like these other gang's do in these prisons and on the street. We also don't get into the prison politics. We are neutral. We have no allegiance to no one but GBG members and other Gays. We have no alliance to any groups. Our adversaries are anyone who feels the need to treat my kind wrongly and the police. And honestly speaking our dislike for the policy is only induced because they have arrested most of us and those quarrels are a host within our own selves. "What race that Gay dudes normally have the most problem with?" I asked.

"Who else do you think? The damn Southern Mexicans and that is only when a Mexican homosexual hit the. They don't like for a Mexican to be gay, they say it is a disgrace to the Mexican race, and under no circumstances they are allowed to walk the yard. See that shit had caused a full fledge war with GBG's, which brought the Blacks, others and Northerner Mexicans to back our play against the Southern Mexicans and the white's. "Why is that?" I asked. For one the GBG, being that there are different races in the

Gay Boy Gangsters and when they see the Gays getting down with the Southern Mexican all they saw was the other races fighting and stabbing Southern Mexicans and the other races took fight and it was an all-out war. There are only designated yards were Mexican homosexuals could walk without their life being in immediate danger by the Southern Mexicans. "How men in prison become gay". I asked.

Well some of them already been gay but just been in the closet. Then you have those who like to indulge in the sexual pleasures as top or just like getting some head, and they think because they are not getting fucked, that don't make them gay. The formal identity would be bisexual, but the facts stands on its own merits they are gay but just in denial. I cannot give you a correct answer to the question. I can only tell you of what I assume and witnessed on several different occasions. I have seen men come into the prison with feminine ways that are weak physically and get turned out. You have duties in here who, looks for those types especially for the young men who come to prison for the first time that has no sense of awareness, easily persuaded, intimidated by fear of the unknown and vulnerable to any deceptive, illusory friendly smile and comforting shoulder. They become the victims of sexual assaults who end up submitting to the ways of life as a homosexual for the protection and that emotional shield of feeling safe. I know because I am one of those vultures who like turning out the young men who come to prison. I like the feisty ones. I'm not into the raping, but I am a master and big participant in alluring and persuading my prey to indulging into my prey to indulging into my sexual pleasures and once they do and feel comfortable with me then I make my move to break in that young virgin booty whole. There is no un-doing down once I let them crawl all up in me for free. They are going to give it up or it is going to be some serious problems.

"I thought you said you were not into raping? I asked.

"I am not. I don't see that as rape. I see it as a fair trade. I give them some of my pussy in return for some of that young ass. A fair trade is not a robbery and if I have to clip a chin to get my issue than that's what a bitch has to do, but I am going to get mine. I call it a favor for a favor and if they are men, they shouldn't be going up in me in the first place. In prison a person has two choices no in between. You either a predator or a prey and you have to remember prison is not temporary place for me it's my home and I have to be as comfortable as possible and every chance there's an opportunity that I can crawl up in something tight and young that come to prison I am going to and I am not the only one who thinks like this. We have the real booty bandits running around the yards that are waiting to catch him some fresh meat to knock out and drag up into his room. Sometimes all you have to do is get them high on some Black Girl. If they never did drugs before they are going to be super high. There wouldn't be any strong resistance then. It's just like taking candy from a baby then."

"Do homosexuals have to be housed with another homosexual?" I asked.

"No, classification cell's everyone up by their ethnicity and with a member from the same gang you are from. If you are part of a gang and they don't have any open cells to house you with one your members they would house you with a non-affiliate this also could become a problem there is no such thing as non-affiliates with some guys come to the prison and say they are not affiliated with any gang when the truth is they are part of a gang but just don't want the administration to know about it. The problem starts when a person is assigning to a cell with a non-affiliate when in all actuality, they are a gang member or affiliates, or he might be one of your rivals. Plus, prison gangs have, rules that none of their members are to be housed up with homosexual."

"Also, life is no joke it is nothing to be taken lighting you can lose your life at any giving moment for no reason at all someone could just wake up in bad move and want to stab someone, and you just might be the one who he picks."

9

WOOD'S

"What is the Wood Pile?" I asked.

"We are regular Woods, white boys who believe in white pride. We are branch from our big bro's in white pride. We are a branch from our big bro's Aryan Brother "The Brand" we call ourselves the Wood Pile because of the number of woods we have in the family and when we come for that as we are coming in a pile, in a big number. We are not racist like the skins or the N.L.R.; we are just for our people the superior white race. We love ourselves.

"What is the difference between the wood pile and other white gangs? "I asked. We are more laid back; we not are into doing hard time and always looking for something to get into. We just want to kick back do our dope go to the visit and see the old lady, finger bang the cunt a little, fuck with who we choose to fuck with score for some dope, and keep a smooth program going. We are not into cutting our hair all bald. Some of us like it long. We do not follow other people ways. That's why we do what we choose to buy our dope from who has the clove at the time when we run out. We don't give a damn what color they are. Dope is dope as long as it's good there are no complaints. The skin heads run their little program like they are in a military school, to many rules, wrinkled mad dog faces and seem to always have something to prove. They keep their head shaved to inform other woods who they are. They don't buy or deal with the

Afrikan Amerikan. They have a straight hate for Afrikans and Mexicans and mainly anyone that's not white, but the especially don't like Afrikans and they feel all whites should. If you are not in agreement with their belief's you basically made an enemy, but the skins are under us. When it comes to the wood pile and the skins, we will regulate to put them back in their place. I do not know wood like skins we only accept them because they are our people and also my big bros requested that we keep the peace between us. The skins are also the Brands extension of military to be sent on missions that needs to be handled, but we have gone to war, and it was an ugly sight on bother ends. Their numbers are large as well and still growing The N.L.R. they are our comrades well was I should say until my big bros stamp them with the Green light. Lately we haven't been killing each other and that's because we all needed to stick together to deal with the problems with other races to keep our numbers strong, but the N.L.R.'s seems to always be on a death wish, they just love trouble and keeping tension in the air. They used to be the brands side arms before they start trying to take over the California prisons. I give them they do they have taking over a lot of yards in call that is and time from time we do war. The Wood Pile members are huge that reaches out nationwide. Some programs are man differently than others, but we are the Wood Pile.

"When a new Wood comes to prison what are the first thing the Woods do?" first he would be approached and questioned who he is, where he is from. We want to know his full name, were he lives, what gang he represents, what he is locked up for and how much time he is doing. We need to read his paper work with the charges on it. We need to make sure he is no Chester. We don't allow rapist or Chester's to walk the yards. We kill them right on the spot. Sometimes we may even fuck them first and stick a mop handle and some other objects up his ass before slicing the cock suckers throat. If we are tweaking off some meth, we will experiment with him. Tie him up stick him under the bed or tape a freak book to his back, grease him up and go to town. We let the rapist see how it feels to have some wood up in him. It had been times when we let a rapist walked the yard because he had a big money and the Woods agreed so we could get the money. We had him believing that we under stood what he done, was just a mistake and we are offering him a chance to clean it up by paying rent. Once we tap his money service then we send him out in a body bag. A lot of my wood comrades wouldn't care how much money a Chester had and what we could milk him out of they want blood on a knife right then and there no exception. However if the wood come into the system and he is clean Then we set him up with a care package, but we do expect the things we issue him to be returned whenever he makes it to the canteen, but if a wood comes in and he is a lame we will take him under the wings and tax him and if we don't. The N.L.R. or the skins will. We normally look for the youngsters to come into the system so we could school our soldiers to be sent on missions. We pump their small minds up with the white pride teachings with an understanding that the white race is the superior of all others. We tell them whatever they do, do it for white pride the Wood Pile. The teachings normally get them pumped up along with a line or two of meth straight to the brain that gets them wired up ready for action and give them heart to tackle any task bravely. "How does the Wood Pile make money inside the prisons?" I asked.

Just like everyone else, sell a little dope here and there and party with the rest. We have different hustles. Some do tattoo work, make wine, draw portraits and cards, fix appliance, sell food from the kitchen, tax lames do legal work. There are a lot of different hustles we do to make an end. It all depends on what type of trade you have or what you like doing. Me, I like giving orders to other Woods and collecting my share of the dope that is brought in and go shoot me a nice shot of dope and tweak off of making picture frames out of potato chip bags or play dungeon and dragons with my cellmate, but I have a lot of comrades who hustles consistently with nothing but working fags and women out of money. They play those internet circuit web sites, placing personal Ad's on them for pen pal and romance. When they write they sell them a lot of dreams and a lot of them fall for the lies that's being told and send money, packages, magazines, books, basically whatever is being asked of them. The fags really paid well. I even have about seven that I write to. Most fags are easily picking's, all they want is for you to write them letters with wild sexual prison fantasies and they run with it. They love that shit and pay to keep it coming. All you need is a hand full that is dishing out from twenty-five to fifty dollars a month; a wood could live comfortably inside the prison. It is all fair you want to play you must pay.

"Does the Wood Pile have a mandatory work out?" I asked.

It's mandatory for all Woods to work out. It is request that every Wood put in two hours

Of activity in every day, bar work, calisthenics or road work. It doesn't matter it is a must we stay fit to some degree. As long as a Wood stay in shape enough to swing a bone crunches swiftly without being winded then that's all that matters. The size of our knives makes up the difference of what we have deprived our bodies physically. Too many of us Woods like to party, it's a common fact that we enjoy using dope. As long as it is around, we going to continue to use. We Woods do not have any shame in our game. We are hogs, Vikings and down for our dirt.

"How does the Wood Pile view the police?" I asked.

"We all hate the god dam pigs, fuck them all in their asses with a black dick nark mother fucker. It would be nice if we inmates could just all come together and kill all those bastards, but there are so many under cover rats amongst the inmates. We would be rated out before the groups could put something together as massive like that in the California prisons in the high security level 4's. All the prison gangs have come to an agreement when a pig hurts an inmate each race has to stab a pig and that's how it's been going down. It's prisoner's law now, between the whites Mexicans and blacks. The others, those pieces of shits aren't going to do nothing but tuck their tails and conform to prison rules. I hate those foreign sons of bitches. They always got their noses up the pig's ass. That's why we keep our foot on their necks and make them pay to stay on the yards. They pay well also, and they come in handy when we Woods are on lock down and can't make it to canteen. We just send them to the canteen to get what the wood pile needs. They know not to deny us, or we would wreak havoc on their parade and rape their cells of anything of value when we come off lock down. My people don't see eye to eye with the pigs. We give them mutual respect and stay out their way. We have a policy and that not to get friendly with no pigs unless it's one who's committing felonies for the pile, bring in the dope sack, and even then we would stab his ass if we had to: There are only two things that we really give a shit about and that's keeping the white race strong and our dope.

"Does the Wood Pile have any other allegiance with other gang's in prison other than white?" I asked.

The Surenos who are the Southerner Mexicans, South Siders, whatever you want to call them. We have an understanding with them. It's been established many moons ago that against the blacks. They catch our backs and we catch theirs. The northerner Mexicans rides with the blacks so any time we clash heads with either group we know that most likely we will have problems with both, the other race just going to wait in the cut to jump in. But that's the same way with us and the surenos. There are only four main races that run the prisons and that are whites, Southerners, Northerners and Afrikan Amerikan.

The Surenos and the Wood do have our little problems with each other and clashes heads mainly over dope. A Wood might not want to pay up or his money didn't make it on time and a Surenos want to tax a Wood. Plus, it is over a power struggle. Every race wants the top rank the power and respect and controlled the drug flow in the prisons. We white know we are better than all other races and everyone should bow down and conform to our rules. The Southerners feel the same way about themselves and I don't know if the northerners and Black fell that way or not and honestly don't care how they feel, all I know is that the white race is superior in my eyes. "Does Rape take place inside the prison?" I asked.

"Of course, it does, there are people who get their booty hole getting took from time to time. A true Wood is not going to let no other man take his man hood. A true Wood rather die first before that happen. Those that get raped are a weak links from the start and deserve to have their booty hole tampered with if he is not going to stand up for themselves. I   hate to admit it and I'm not ashamed to do so, but in the wood pile. We do have some cold-hearted woods who are booty bandits to the bone. And I am sure every race has them. We can't disown them; they are some solid woods who have earned their bolts righteously with honor. They might end up raping a lame who he been getting high with. It is common for a wood to treat a lame to a good shot of dope and then want to fuck him or get a spit shine. The wood pile is nothing nice. We insane to the brain, barbarians by nature and wicked by circumstances especially when we use white sinister, it brings the demon out you your Horne as a bessy bug, woods get tired of pulling on himself. Some of us need that friction those tight pale white cheeks if you know what I mean? "Don't Woods have wives; girl friends are they ever thought about before doing just inhuman acts to another man?" I asked.

"Yeah a lot of us has old ladies but most of the run off when a Wood get locked down. Sancho take our places. They start slacking on their obligation and playing games. Letters slow down, money stop coming in, phone call being refused. So, who gives a shit about what a tramp thinks? They can't even hold strong for a Wood when he's down. There is a poem that the Wood send their old ladies when she had enough of their bull shit. It goes like this.

As I sit here on my bunk
with nothing to do.
I think of the punk that's fucking you.

He knows of me

But yet still he clowns.

So, his time will come

To be shot down.

I am able to do it quickly

I know I could.

But killing him fast

is far too good.

I'll grab your sancho

by his hair.

You'll see my anger

I no longer care.

I'll beat him down

Till my heart's content.

Till his miserable life

aren't worth a cent.

I'll put my six guns

unto his head

squeeze five times

until he's dead.

There's one shot left

this is true

this one I have saved

especially for you.

So, watch your back bitch

You and sancho are through.

When I get released, I am fucking him too.

I hope this hurt

And makes you cry,

Because I know you'll be a tramp

Till the day you die.

This poem ends with me in my cell.
So good bye, fuck you
And see you in hell.

"Yeah that is how it done. It's been floating from prison to prison. I don't even know who wrote it, but whoever wrote it was feeling just like a lot us do when the old lady moves on with her life. They always end up coming back when they think you are about to go out. Who wants a bitch that can't stay strong for her man? Those are the tramps when you get out you run thought and let your comrades fuck. Then you dog the shit out of her. Get her strung out on dope and do all the worse that is possible and leave her. I tell all my comrades who ladies leave them how to do her when they get out and some do just that, and a few stays with the tramp and don't follow the plan.

"What type of advice would you give those who have not been to prison? I asked.

"I would tell them to stuff a load of dope up their asses and come on to prison. No, I am just bull shiting around about that. There is only one, way I can say it, and that's in a poem, but after this I must be going. I waste enough time with you and your book.

In this place of concrete valley flowers and streams of pipe
and rust,
There is no man in this man-made hell that you can count on or
trust. You may think sitting in that ill cell is such a bore or drag.

But let me tell you something, friend I'd rather be here than in a
body bag.

For when that cell door comes to an open you enter the real
world of bitter fate.

You make your way to the yard and smell the stench of
pure hate.

You see it in the eyes of those who have become stagnant
by the system if you don't watch you every action you will
become their next victim.

You live and dwell in this hate long enough and you may
even taste it sometime or other it may be someone you've never
met or someone you take as brother.

So now you heard the story my friend the story of a place
called prison take heed and make the best of life my friend for
you don't want to enter the belly of the beast.

To all my comrades and solid Woods stay strong for
twenty-three that represent superior woods.

10

UNITED BLOOD NATION
(UBN)

"Tell me who are the UBN and were they come from?" I asked.

"We are Blood's, Blood gang members from different hoods from all over the world, who has union into one solid organization. That is why we call ourselves United Blood Nation. We are one humongous family who has a common interest to prosper, to be successful, to be the most powerfulness force on the streets and to hold important positions in the cosmopolitan arena. What people don't know is we are not into gang banging. We are far from that foolishness, it is senseless, un productive and plain stupid to be killing over colors property that don't belong to any of us or over meaning less exchange of words. We UBN'S do not engage ourselves into such ignorance of the unnecessary or participate in any thing that is in conducive to our aspirations."

"The UBN was started in the California prison system by my home boy who's originally from PDL. It was established to bring all the blood set's that was in the California prison system together as one. To eliminate feuding between us and to bring the blood love back that had been lost by small disputes that could have been easily worked out. And to stay as a solid foundation to protect all bloods from adversaries. The UBN'S was only looked at as a prison gang until my home boy who started the UBN got with the other home boy who is doing time in a Nevada Maximum State Prison to bring all the blood's out there in the prison's together under the UBN. He had a vision and concept of establishing something much bigger thing much bigger than just a UBN prison gang. Being that he had life and was the leader of the play boys blood gang out in Vegas and had a younger relative who was incarcerated that was about to hit the streets who was also a blood, a top rank Peru, who was dependable, trust worthy and loyal. The homie gave his relative the script to what he wanted done and his blessings and his relative made the United Blood Nation what they are today, a world-wide organization that's on the streets and inside the prisons, that's how we really became about.

The criminal activities that we involve ourselves in are for a financial gain to support the Blood Nation. To send the home boy's and home girls to college and trade schools to build legal businesses, to build safe houses in every state, to support the homies that's looked up financially and to pay for legal representation when one of our members need it. Our goal is to have a UBN in every professional field of employment. That's why we send some of our members to college to get those college degrees. We want to have a link and access to whatever we need. We have members who have different functions. Everyone doesn't get down and dirty with the street life. We find out what type of talent each member has and that becomes their required duty and obligation to our family. We have crews who do nothing but robberies, push dope, boosters, checks and credit card fraud, scheme on insurance companies, file fake taxes with the IRS, and then we have our assassin crew. This crew is the elite of the UBN they are called the untouchables. They are silencers majority of the UBN members will never know who the members of the untouchable are. The reason for that is to limit any possible betrayal of a UBN member who might turn law and disclose the identity of this crew who does the killing for the UBN. The less they know the less they can speak about. The only people who would know who an untouchable is an untouchable and the captain of the UBN. Everyone else is blind to their identity. The untouchables are our silencers. They don't hang out with the homie boys, they keep a low key, there style of dress is classy, and most of them will not have tattoos with any indication that would link them to belonging to a group or gang. They socialize and intermingle with everyone to keep the ability to infiltrate. If an untouchable come to prison, he would most likely be classified as a non-affiliate and house with another non-classified as a non-affiliate and house with another non-affiliate or a gang member. This person who he might be housed with might be an enemy of the bloods, but the untouchable would never expose his hand or show any hostility or aversion he would be friend the enemy, eat, laugh and joke with the enemy, to mislead and gain the enemy trust. The untouchable will find out who has the keys on the yard for the bloods and if there is any UBNS there, if the key holder is not a UBN the untouchable will not deal with the bloods on the yard. If they key holder is a UBN then the untouchable would call to the streets to do a check on this UBN member once he gets conformation that the UBN key holder is a captain, then he would pull him to the side and introduce him selves. The UBN would not tell the other blood members that there is an untouchable on the yard he would just inform the bloods that he has a relative on the yard and he is not a blood but to catch his back if he gets into any trouble. The untouchable that's on the yard would become a great informative source for the bloods because he would be in a position to hear things that wouldn't normally be spoken around blood members.

The untouchables originated out of Vegas when the homie relative got out of prison he put much foot work in to building the UBN. It takes a certain type of blood to be part of our family, not just any body is allowed into the UBN family. Like for instance I said we are strengthening our selves and building for the future so all UBN members can live well. We don't have time for hard heads, loose cannons who want to gang bang and bring heat on the family. We keep those types of bloods at a distance. We try to avoid having and dealings with them and it must be, or we will eliminate them. We don't have time to be dealing with the envy, jealousy, resentful, bitterness and ill feelings of other's, we don't like in house problems and those who don't like to follow instruction, but always like to give them. That's why we try to choose are members carefully. All of the UBN members are consider leaders. It is just there are some who hold higher rank then others. UBN is not about competing with each other; it is about achieving a common goal for a better livelihood.

We have some bloods who choose to do their own thing and that's Bool with us. As long as they keep it blood love and not try to harm or put any UBN members in harm's way then there will be no problem, but regardless inside the prisons if you are a blood but not a UBN, we will still have his back. We look out for Bloods and we are not going to let no one hurt one of ours who is claiming this red madness. We also discipline our own, if any of ours step out of pocket. We don't allow for no other group or race to put their hands on a blood especially a Nation. All bloods might not feel like us or might not assist us, but that's Bool because we UBNS going to keep it real and Backing and looking out even if the love is not shown back. That is how we run our program, because when it all boils down to a Blood it is a Blood in the eyes of the enemy.

In the prisons UBN's push a hard line. We have rules that must be followed, and mandatory work out program. No using any drugs other than bud, and not to come to the yard drunk are you will be chastised severely. There is absolutely no indulging in homosexual activities, or we will blast you out your boots, we have no understanding when it comes to that gay shit. We only cell up with Blood's. If you are not a Damu up, when new Blood comes to the yard, we get at him to see what set he's from and a few other basic questions like his name, and were he comes from. We don't go through let me see your paper work stuff. If you Blood is foul, he should already know how we get down, or we will blast him. So, Blood that is not right is not going to be walking the main line. We will find out if there is any smut on him. We do our investigation on later days. We make sure the Bloods that come in have what they need. New clothes, shoes, television, food, hygiene and what every else they need to get on their feet. It's mandatory that we stay looking fresh in our appearance and stay groom and smelling good. We have a lot of young knuckle heads and wild bloods that come through these prisons with their pants hanging down to their knees like them crips, and we have to immediately put a stop to that. We do not wear saggy our pants. We have style in our way of dressing. When a little homie come throw, we school him on the rules first, what's permissible and what's not because if he goes and does something and get caught up into some shit this affects the whole blood car. So, we make sure they are taught right on the laws of prison, the rules of the blood family and the ways on how he is expected to conduct himself, if he doesn't have his high school diploma, his ass is going to school. It's not going to be no hanging out kicking it with the fam bam when you got school business to take care of. We keep a tight leash on the young ones we don't misuse our little homies like a lot of gang's do. We strengthen our weak; we educate our illiterate and help those who seem to have lost their caricature find it. We motivate the slacker's because we know what we pass down to them through our love and teaching, they will pass down to another little homie some day and the blood line would stay strong and positive. We do send little homies on missions. They have to learn by experience, because when a war kicks off with the blood and who ever. They will have to be accounted for. We are not holding no hand's they were man enough to do whatever they done to come to prison, they are man enough to stand up as a man. We just make sure they got their proper schooling, but we always got they back. When a blood wants to become a UBN and we decide that he's worthy. He has to blast someone out his boots. If he was to become a UBN on the street, he would have to dome someone. We don't go around killing or harming innocent people. Our targets are fore legitimate reasons. We have a no exception rule when it comes to kids and old folks. They are not to be harmed under any condition. In the prison it is mandatory that all UBN's be up out of bed by time breakfast is announced and there is no sleeping until the entire program is shut down, if they are caught sleeping in their cell during the day they will be disciplined. It is mandatory that all UBN's keep their cells clean and neat. We also have a kitty were extra items is kept for the new arrivals who need a few things or if one of the homies run out of something, he can just get it out of the kitty. It's also recommended that all UBN's stay stocked up on hygiene's and to have an emergency supply of food, coffee and tobacco in their cell just in case the prison go on long lock downs we won't be hurting for anything.

On every yard there is a blood that brings in the sack, and all the UBN's get an issue to slang for canteen. The UBN's don't have3 to sell drugs in the prison. We normally do it because the money come in the abundance, plus it allows us to save the money that is on our books for emergencies purposes if we ever go to Ad-Seq or the SHU security housing unit. Plus, a lot of homies like blowing that tweed and they going to make a way to get it. So, we might as well get the rest of the goods and send our customers to the store for us and at the same time make that money and contribute to our cause. The woods love that heroin and speed. If you have either of   the two and it's good, they will spend. We look out for the ones who spend with us. It keeps them coming back spending their money with Blood's, because they know we will deal straight up and show love. The Indians on the yards also love that heroin and money best customers are the Asians. They like that crack and majority of the Asians who are in prison normally have money or an outside source they get money from. You will normally never have a problem collecting from an Asian because they don't want any trouble especially from the Blood's. Here in prison when there is an individual problem with two different fractions it just doesn't only involve them personally but the entire two groups. So, say if the Asian couldn't pay we take it to his people and let them know about it and the dept would be on them to pay. If they refuse, then we take off on all the Asian's. That goes for any group or race but like I said they money is good as well as the south side Mexicans who claim they don't fuck with blacks on business. That bull shits. If we got heroin and they hear that it's the bomb they will send another or a wood to come buy the dope from us or they will just pull one of the home boys to the side and deal business on the under. A dope fiend is a dope fiend, I don't care about what type of racial shit they are going through. They are going to go get that dope to keep the monkey off their back simple as that. We don't even trip on their politics, because we don't care nothing about them, as long as we get our money and they respect us then there is no problem, but soon as they cross those lines we will take off on them, but one thing I can honestly say about them south side Mexican's although they got they little racist shit going on. They are respectful regardless what they may feel inside about you. If you get into an argument with one of them ask for a head up fade. They will not fight any black head up, but they will try to jump you. At least with the crips you can get a head up fade to avoid a mass riot. Some crips will honor the challenge and some won't but most will. We won't sell any crack to any Afrikan Amerikans. That is asking for a problem, plus we know a lot of blacks in prison don't have the type of money to be buying in crack at the penitentiary prices that it's sold for. A ten-dollar street value of crack is sold for fifty bucks. Afrikans like that bud and that's where the money is at when it comes to selling drugs to them. It might come eight to ten dollars at a time for a cap, but it comes daily and continuously with a huge cliental. All UBN's are under paper work which is an oath that is pledge to the United Blood Nation. The same way you came in is the same way you can get out but with your own life being taken. We are serious about what we believe in and do and if someone thinks they can take us lightly. We will dome him without a second thought. If a member of the UBN ever decides he wants to show resistance and go against us. We will make an example out of his family one at a time until we could get him. We will start killing his immediate family members. Although we have no exception to the rule about harming kids and old folks, but that exception is bent when it comes to anything that is a treat to the UBN'S. If a kid is older enough who could distinguish facial features, we wouldn't let that kid live, for the simple fact it could come back to hunt a member if the kid could give a description and identify the person, they seen do harm to someone. No witnesses would be left that is able to talk and point fingers. This is only to protect the UBN and its members, when it comes to us and our safety and wellbeing. There are no rules to the game other than to do whatever it takes to keep the family from harm when you become an Untied Blood Nation. We become your immediate family and everything else is secondary to us. I mean everything, if someone does something harmful to a UBN, we will do everything in our power to get him. We don't care what that is we must get revenge. I stress that strongly anything. That's just how it goes to show the loyalty and love for our extended family. There are members who don't see eye to eye or even like each other but they know not to let their personal dislikes get in the way of the loyalty that all members are entitled to. All the UBN's don't know each other because we are so big and we are all over in different states, plus we don't have any UBN hoods. We have safe houses and our family who over sea's the safe house in their state will inform other UBN member's in that state that there is a relative in town and someone will come and escort him around to meet the others. We don't broadcast the Nation it's kept on the hush. We don't mark walls and buildings up with the family name. Our thing is to stay low keyed and productive. In the prison system we are not the only Blood Gang. There are a lot of them, but we are by far the biggest and extend out into every state. We are the Dogg Pound and when push comes to shove, we make the decisions for all the bloods or we will take fight on those who don't want to follow in line.

Although crips are enemies of the Bloods for no other reason than they are a different gang that represents a different color, and many years of ill feelings and intense dislike for pass act's and killings we have been doing to each other regardless of our differences, when the Afrikans have a problem with another race all Afrikans come together and deal with it. In the prisons we ride together when it affects the Afrikan race. All Afrikans gangs have that understanding and if a group of Afrikans don't assist they will be dealt with by all the other groups of Afrikans. In the prisons we try to keep all the fighting out between the Afrikans. When there is a problem, we try to deal with it reasonably without violence. The Afrikans also have alliances who, roll with the black's, the Northern Mexican's, Northenos, those are our Dogg's. We fuck with them in a big way. A lot of them were raised up with Afrikans; they are totally different from the south side Mexican's. The Northerner's have style. They also rep the same color as we do, them fools stay flamed up. They kicked and act just like we do. They don't wear their heads shaved bald like them sewer rats south side Mexican's. On the streets and the prison's, we ride together. The Southside's don't like that, but they can't do nothing about it, and if they try, we just going to blast a bunch of them out of their boot's. The Northerner's are no punks they know how to sling them Dogg's from the shoulder's just like Afrikan do and they will do some stabbing with the quickness. The Southsider's are already enemies on the streets, so basically, we all have the same enemies. The crips really don't care to much about the North side Mexicans because they favor bloods more plus their color is red, but they don't trip with them, and we are not going to except it. This prison life shit is Brazy, but this is our reality and if a person can't overlook it his life could come to end quickly. Doing time is not the lick; this shit will drive a person in sane. It causes you to move swing, be sad, depress, angry just because you are tired of being locked up, and just tired of being tired. You get tired of eating the same old' shit especially soups, seeing the same old' faces, hearing the same stories, doing the same thing, going through the same problems, and dealing with the same issues. Ever thing is the same the only difference is it's another day just like the others. Peoples trying to stay high or drunk to escape from this place trying to hold onto the little sanity they might still have. Being locked up make you forget how to be human, you always on your guards, always forming a negative opinion about a person. The vision to the outside world is lost. You begin to look at things in a different way than you would have if you were on the streets. Ugly women begin to look good to you, women that you wouldn't have given a second glance, you begin to cherish and become over protective over petty things like magazines, books, tapes, a soup, T-shirts, you name it and some, inmates will try to actually kill you over a soup or magazine. It is not good to let other inmates use your property. I am not speaking about my UBN family we share it all because it's nothing to us, but I am speaking in general. Some inmates will let an inmate use a book or magazine, and when it's return, he will remove a page and step to the inmate who he let use the magazine and request to be paid for the magazine because a page is missing. Regardless how much the inmates try to convince the other that he didn't take any pages out. That is irrelevant the other inmate already knows that he is just gaming to come up on a few ends. If the other inmate refuses to pay, it will be a big issue and most likely somebody will be stabbed. These are some of the game's inmates play and there are a lot of them. Now if that guy doesn't have the money to pay then the other inmate would demand something, like some ass, head, and dinner trays. It's always a hidden motive when an inmate pulls moves like this. Prison time is more than just physical it's also mental and that the hardest part is doing the mental time, if you can do the mental the rest is a piece of cake.

11

SKIN HEADS

What are skin heads? I asked.

"A collection of superlative white men standing strong for the superior white race, we are white supreme white race. We are the white supremacy, National Socialist. We are the white force of Hail Hitler, Nazis. We do not believe in democracy unless its representatives are white supremacy. We support the white race only. We believe in superiority, racist to all coloreds, creed and the government. One of our goals is to recruit as many white men as possible and give them the teachings of our superior race and build a military to take over the streets and run all the prisons. Once we can accomplish this goal, we will free all whites and pack the prisons with Niggers, Kikes, Nips, and Hat dancers who are the light skin Niggers with straight hair, and feed them one meal a day, pull out all the televisions, radios, and slave them hard. We didn't start out in any prisons. Nazi skin heads were organized in society. We have Nazis support groups, Web sites, Newspapers, businesses and other sources of advocates for us skins. We are unlike other groups who people don't back there play and support them. In these prisons we skin train physically. We study the teachings of our heritage, the history of the superior race. We keep our heads shaved bald and advertise our Swazi tattoo's proudly. To inform all other races that we are Nazi Skin Heads the superior race. We look down on everyone that is not white and even the whites that are not in conformity with our actions. We do not socialize or do business with other races our words are limited to mutual respect, but on the surface of our hearts we feel other races don't deserve to be respected. Why respect them when they disrespect themselves. Prime example the niggers, look at the way they wear their clothes down pass their big asses, their hair in girly pony tails trying to walk cat cool looking like apes. When they speak, the words that come out their mouth sounds distorted, may be its because of those big lips they have but whenever you can understand what they are saying it be something ignorant. They also disrespect themselves and their race, but one thing we skins due respect, admire and applaud them for. Is the fact they are killing off their own race. I love to hear when another nigger done shot and killed another nigger in a drive by shooting. I love to see their baby apes walking around dirty and living in filth and their parents are strung out on crack cocaine. I love when the illiterate apes kill each other over poverty-stricken government land that don't even belongs to them, they kill each other over red and blue, they degrade and sell their women apes, give them HIV. This is what we admire about them. As long as they continue the excellent work of killing off their own. That saves us the pleasure of killing them off our selves. We skin just get so tired hearing them bickering about the white man keeping them down the white man this, the white man that, he is the oppressor. It is not our fault that we are the superior race and the Apes are killing and oppressing themselves. The more we give them to pacify their winning the more they want. We gave free money and housing, food stamps, television stations, books, and even a full month to do their little bull shit apes memorialize festivities of the mud baby history. What history? They don't have any history. Yes, we hate them because our ancestors hated them, and it is in our genes. We are just keeping the white tradition alive.

We feel the same way about those hat dancers the Mexicans are nothing but light skinned niggers with straight hair who run across the border to our land and have a small army of hat dancers that can't speak English and contaminate our societies with filth. The only reason we put up with them in the prison is due to the other white gangs. They asked us to try to keep the peace. The south side Mexicans and the whites have an agreement that they will assist each other to fight against the ape niggers. That's agreement has been established way before my time. We skin feel that we need no one to back our play. We can hold our own we don't help the hat dancers when they are at war with the niggers.

The other whites sometimes do but not the skins. Why help, when we really want to see both races dead or screaming in pain for their lives. What they are doing is doing us a favor killing each other.

We have a lot of skins coming into the prison these days our numbers are continuing to grow. When a skin pulls up, he basically knows the protocol. To let it be known were he comes from who was on the yard with him his name, charge, how much time he is doing. We set him up; school him about what's been happening on the yards, and who holds the keys for the skin's and introduce him to everyone. If a none skin comes throw, we try to be the first to pull him to the side for questioning, because he might be a good white to recruit as a skin if h is a lame then we will tag him so the other whites would know he is our mark and we will tax him. If he doesn't have any money, we will use him as our lackey or have him to hand wash our clothes or hold on to our knives. We will find something for him to do and he will submit to our request or we will not hesitate to bash his face in. We are most definitely into extortion. It is not that we need the money we just like applying pressure on lames that are not making a contribution to cause of the white empowerment over all races and creeds. Believe me if we don't pressure the lames someone else will out the white race. We also don't care about the age of the lame young, in the middle or old. They going to pay or catch hell. One thing about us skins we don't care about going to war. We thrive off the feeling of danger. The adrenalin rush is so fascinating better than any high you can get from a drug. Its more than mind blowing to the extremist of the insane it is pure personified evil at its best. I guess that's the mentality you take on when being in prison for a while you must learn how to be the best hater it is, and we are good at that. We used to assist the Aryan brother hood's and Aryan warriors I am doing their dirty work until we realize they were just using us, and we start pushing our own line and going against the grain, to focus on nothing but doing Nazi skin head work. They tried to push the prison politics on us, but it failed and diminished away like a water vapor when they see we would rebel every time and take flight, no matter win, lose or draw. Now if it's not about 88 we don't want any parts of it. 88 are the skins number the double H that stands for Hail Hitler. When we see a comrade, we greet him by saying eighty-eight. The Eight letter of the Alphabet is an H, so we say eighty-eight to give the two H's. All skins must get their colors. You must stab a Jew, Nigger ape, hat dancer or a Rapist. That's how you earn your Swazi and every time you stab a Nigger one of the letters or eights are shaded in. To be a Nazi skin head you must be pure white, there is no half mix white mutt's going to be skin. Its pure white always right. We feel for a white to mix races they had to be weak from the start and their son is week because he had been bred by a weak minded white and a weak race. We are against inter racial relationships each race should stay with their own, and we are against slavery when it consists of having nigger's living on white land, cooking their meals and cleaning white folk homes. We are against that it's too close for comfort.

"What about drugs do the skin head use drugs? "I asked.

A lot of us use drugs and a lot of us don't. I myself like smoking glass. I can get a lot done off that drug. It keeps me up for three to four days at a time. When I am tweaking, I create some of my best drawing and knives. The knives I make are detailed with designs even the plastic one's. The skins got their dope connect. We bring in our own and spread it out among us skins we only sell to the other woods no other race. Mainly the dope we get in is for personal use only to take straight to the neck. We are no into trying to become rich from selling dope in the prison like a lot of those niggers are. When we get out dope, we do sling enough to get a nice issue of canteen a little money and that is about it. Selling dope in the prison is too much of a hassle. It is already too much of a hassle getting it back into the yards. We got to watch the video cameras, the police, and rats and there rat family members because some inmates family members who be on the visits spot someone keistering dope they go rat you out, and then the police want to put you on potty watch or go have x-rays taking to see if you got something, and normally an inmate visitor should have stop them from running to the police. It's easy to find out who told on you because they have to do a report on you, and if there is someone who's working in the program office like an inmate who normally does and does all the typing for the police then he will blow the cover. As so if criminal charges going to be filed on you and district attorney picks up the charges you have to get discovery package, and the names of the person or people would have to be disclosed inside the discovery package. Believe it or not there are a lot of undercover rats on the yards and they run with the gang's ride when it is time to ride and do all the dirt that an inmate can do inside the prison, but they will still rat you out. You have all type of guys in there that does all type of weird shit. They will drop kites on you get an inmate they don't like or want off the yard and is afraid to stab him. They would just drop a kite on him to the police with some bogus bull shit. I even seen some go so far as to sliding a knife in an inmate's room when he was not here and doped a kite. When to police go search his room and find the knife, they roll the inmate up and place him in Ad-Seq under investigation. It is all different kinds of tricks inmates play. That's why you have to stay up on everything and don't trust anyone; you never know what goes through the minds of individuals who have ill feeling and motives. The name of this game is survival and at any giving time your closes comrade could switch up on you and take your life. There are all types' o reason people do what they do. Most guys in here want to be recognized as someone important, feared, admired, and respected. The very thought of achieving that status motivates them into doing whatever it takes to get other inmates to view him as all those things. The reality of it all none of that means anything to a man. There are thousands of hard-core killers, tough guys who are respected in prison, but it won't change anything when another man feels the need to come after you. A lame who gets fed up being pushed in the corners, treated badly and find the heart to pick up a knife and gut you can take all those titles away from you with the blink of an eye. A knife has no friend, feeling, morals, regrets, or regards to one's status. It is going to assault you as violently as the inmate controlling its course of action. That is why we skins try to keep a tight military and stay alert at all times because you never know who might want to gain a reputation off you. It is easy for an inmate to get illusional.

"What does the Skin Head's think about the police? "I asked.

"We Skins have strict rules. No befriending the police and to only talk to them when it is absolutely necessary. We are not into the games like other groups are, sliding their way y up under an officer to get them to bring them things into the prison. For one that moves can be detrimental to you and your entire military. A person should never lose sight that an officer is an officer. It could just be a set up a sting operation. We skin do have brains. We ponder on things before doing them. We make planes to how we will attack a situation. Dealing with the police is not ever an option that we would consider pondering on. Having any dealings with them is out the question. There is a lot of things that we skin don't agree on that other white gangs do, and we do check them and sometimes have to war with them to get our point across. That is why we are building our military forces up strong so we can do a mass sweep and claim every yard. We skin going to wipe out all other white gangs in the prisons. That's the plan we have mapped out. We thought about bringing a load of dope, and all the skins fill a syringe up with heroin and pick out a white and just plunge the dope into their necks. This was the same plan that we had for the niggers and the hat dancers before we thought about using it for the whites. It hasn't become official as of yet until all skins over the nation agree on doing it. We want to do it in a massive way. We will give the whites a chance to except.

"Do the skins involve them self in rapes of other inmates?" I asked.

Skins do a lot of things that skins shouldn't do. In different prisons the key holder for the skins might give the other skins lee way to do what they feel need to be done at that time. If a situation comes up that needs to be handled the skin that has been sent to handle the problem. He chooses the method of how he wants to approach and take care of the matter how he sees fit. If he chooses to apply some pleasurable anal pain before bringing great bodily harm, then that's what he chooses to do. No one will question it. Sometimes we skin need other ways of harming those who got an issue coming. We do get bored with stabbing someone. So, we think of other things to do like take a person's man hood. That is a slow death in itself. It destroys a person mentally. We like applying this punishment to the rapists, women beater, Chester, and rats. Then we stab them up. It is nothing like to watch and hear a rapist beg and cry for us to stop giving him something that the gave to some unwilling soul. You rape the white race we rape you. You molest the white race we molest you. You harm the white race women we harm you. We will rape you then take all of your belongings.

"Where are the officers when all this raping and stabbing is going on? I asked.

We have skins who would be our pawn do distract the floor officers and keep their attention while we rush up in a cell. We tie up and gag our victims, one forth skins will keep watch, while we do our thing. You would be an amazed how willing many would just bend over without being tied up once they see that bone crusher in your hand. Some officers will turn their backs while we take care of business. There are a lot of ways we successfully get our victims. A lot of the officers that works in these prisons have families and they are not quick to place their own lives in harm way for an inmate if that mean turning their head that's what they will do. Because someone is an officer doesn't make them a law abiding, honest, trust worthy, person. Some who were the badges are criminals who just haven't been caught. The officers are crooked not all of them, but a lot of them and that is what makes the prison even more dangerous because you never know who is helping who, and which officers favoring what race or group. We skin seem to always get lee way with white officers over other race that is just a fact, because we represent for the white race and they see this. We also get a lot of our information from the officers about who are rating, rapist or when the yard is about to be search. A lot of them provide us with such type of information. This happens all the time.

12

CRIP'S

"What is Crip's?" I asked.

A notorious, hostile, unsympathetic, hot tempered and violent black gang who involves themselves into every street criminal activity to make money and to come up on personal wanted merchandise. We are one of the biggest gang's in the world with several thousand different Crip's gangs. We are the blue rags. Even though there are thousands of different Crip's gangs who claim Crip's. We are not altogether. The only thing that makes us known and looked at as one big gang in society eyes is that we all represent the Crip's. There are a lot of gangs that are sole enemies of other Crips gangs everyone doesn't get along and does kill each other over personal dislikes. In these stoop's we try to keep the hostility, and animosity, and personal beefs on the street, and function inside these prison as a Crips family, but my gangsters are crazy, we all are, we be going through some insane wicked and dominating shit. Every hood wants to be the head. It's always some motha fuckers who want to back up from the structure and do they own thing. For some reason we Crips rebels against any type of established authority if it's not our own gang's authority that has been laid down. We like to boss shit, like to be in the lime light, get the recognition and be feared by all other gangs and perceived as being ruthless killers. This is the type of perceptions we have. Shit like that is what's implanted into crips minds, and that be our motivation to go all out and do anything to get this fame, recognition and respect of other gangs. We got those we call OG's (old gangster) who been in the game a long time and has gotten older and a little wiser, know that they are getting old they try to push that soft shit about how we wouldn't be doing this and doing that, but these are the same motha fuckas talking this weak shit who thought us how to be this way that we are today. Plus, that OG title is played out, that shit means nothing to a Crips any more, maybe to a young Crip, but not to one who's been in the game for animate. His ass will get tried, and his reputation taking by a real loc who's not trying to hear that sentimental, heart touching, sympathizing bull shit he's stressing. In the prison the different Crip sets function with their own group but we do have an understanding that we as crips will come together and ride as one. All the Crip gangs have one area that all the crips share. Crips have their work out area, showers, outside bitches, and an elected spokesman. Before the spokesmen can make any decisions for the mass of crips the first must go around to every hood that's on the yard and talk to the head Crip for that group and it is like a voting process. The majority rules, I don't give a dam, it is always going to be a lot of disagreements that is just crips nature. We try to keep a Crip line going without the problems between the Crips. We have so many wild ass young loc's knocking down the prison gates coming in here with a gang of time with no damn sense, gang banging to the follow. We have to snatch their ass by the collar to slow their asses down before they get a lot of shit started without knowing it, because those United Slob Nations is not going to except no disrespect. They will move on a young homie and down him, and then take fight on all crips un-expectantly catching us off guard to what is going down. One thing about them slobs, they are together and will handle their business with any one that cross the lines of respect. I got to give them that much and some of those slob's are cool once you get to know them, but they still slobs are enemies and its Crip with us to the day we die. The problem with us Crips, if a certain Crip fraction gets into it with the slobs' tits not like all the other crips going to help that other Crip gang to fight against the slobs. Some will some won't. I wouldn't say it is out of fear of the slobs but out of deep hatred that a certain Crip gang may have for another Crip gang, and they feel like why we should help them when they are our enemies on the street. So, let them handle they own problem, but it is totally different when it comes to another gang of a different race. A Crip is a Crip then and all crips going to get involved which it will become a race issue and the slobs and all the other black would get into it. When Crip come through those gates, he is asked what set he's from, and if any of his home boys are on the yard. He will be directed to them it becomes their responsibility to place him on what's cracking on the yard, and how the program is running. Every set looks out for their own members and responsible for the action and if cuzz is foul then they must deal with him or someone else will and be ready to lift them for not taking care of their garbage. I have been Crippin a long time and I learned by my own actions and feeling. We can't be trusted, being deceitful is part of our makeup, and we are only loyal to ourselves. We may act though we are loyal to our gang, we will kill, Rob, bang and all the above for our gang, but if push comes to shove that our life and another member life on the line. Then that member is just a dead man we are only reliable when there is some type of personal gain in it for us. That is why those slobs call us crabs because we will pull another Crip down and destroy him to get a head of the game that is a fact. Do you really think we give a fuck about smoking another crip when we go around smoking Niggas, they mommas, bitches, kids and sometimes whole families? Hell no! When you hang around Niggas who do this type of shit you become heartless, uncaring, and unsympathetic for a human life there is no turning around. You going to keep doing whatever you do and try to make sure you stay on top of the game even if that means waling over some of your own members. The game is not like it was back in the days when crips had unity and a purpose. Now the youngsters have put a twist on the game, and they are running the show how they see fit and making the rules as they go.

"So, the crips don't have any rules in the prison?" I asked.

Cuzz listen, I'm going to say it like this. Rules are different were ever you go. Some prisons all the Crips is pushing a Crip line under one set of rules and other prisons crips cars are doing their thing. There are the stander rules about not to be disrespecting other gangs' shit like that, but other than that, crips are pushing their own politics. Don't get me wrong, we do look out for crips in the pen, but there is a limit to that as well. Every Crip car has mandatory work out programs that they do, basically every race for that matter does. Every Crip car tries to get in the dope game, bringing dope into the prisons for sell and to use. You can clock a grip up in this bitch by selling dope to the wood's and if you are fucking with that Black Girl you can make a killing off them sewer rats, lock one of their people in and he will sell to the rest of them. We can't stand them asses though. We are ready to kill them bean burrito eating asses every time we get a chance. On the streets of L.A. We smoke them on a regular basis. Those sewer rats think they better then someone else. They always trying to run shit and pump fear into people, but we don't give fuck about none of that weak shit, we take it to them and let it be known this Crip isn't pushing no line on no crips or blacks for that matter. The sewer rats always with that racial shit, that's why blacks don't like south side Mexicans. The bitches call themselves surenos whatever the fuck that means. They push a hard line on their own people. And in their stoops, they function under one group regardless of what set they are from on the streets. Those fools try to become part of some Mexican Mafia bull shit that's really nothing but a bunch of dope fiends who stay lock down in the SHU's. They don't walk the main line so a real gagster could show them what this Cripping is all about; we will fill their asses up with holes and that on Cripping. If a Crip has funk with a sewer rat, they will not scrap head up. They are too much of a coward to do that, but they will come in a pack with weapons to jump on one person. They don't like us and we sure the fuck doesn't care, and we let it be known that we don't like them by killing them off every time I think about them sewer rates, I get heated. I love it when all the black go to battle against the. We are laying them bitches down, and they be running like hoes. They can save that weak ass shit for their own people or those woods because when they come fucking around with crips they are really playing with death, because we aren't showing no mercy, we will carve that eagle and that mother Mary tattoo or whatever that bitches they be having tattooed on their bodies.

You know the woods are different, we will step to the battle ground and do our thing. After we kick their asses and stab up a few of them. It is like everything is cool again until we battle again. We still sell them dope and fuck with them. Regardless if most are pushing that racist shit, as long as it's not being put out there in the black's face then we don't give a damn what they push. Peck woods are just weird and crazy.

"Can you tell me how you one can become a Crip?" I asked.

Cuzz, that's easy. All Cuzz has to do is say he want to be a Crip and whoever he is hanging, with though crips would jump him in. It's still the same just like it always been when a person is put on the set. It goes down like that in here too. Cuzz even might not have to get knotted up to get on the set, he might just be asked to go stab someone and that would be his initiation.

"How do crips feel about homosexuals?" I asked Cuzz, what you mean how we feel about homosexuals we don't give a fuck about no homosexuals. They are just like everybody else, to be used and abused. Some of the homies do fuck with them in a real way. Celling up with them moth's fuckas and fucking on them and getting sucked up and acting like the punk's are some real bithces and shit. You see some weird shit up in here. Niggas who you never thought that would fuck with punks be dipping around corners fucking with them. Some even let them nasty ass punks put hickies on their necks and chest. I am not with that shit, that shit is gay, and a lot of Crip cars let they home boys get away with dicking down a punk. To be punks are bad luck, but I am not going to sit up here and never say, the thought never crossed my mind of getting some head from one. Some of them gay motha fuckas look just like real bitches, big asses, breast and all. Sometimes you just have to remind yourself them motha fuckas are men and have a long dick between their legs just like you. I have seen some of the little loc get turned out by punks. They call themselves being slick creeping around with the punk. The punks trick them out of the dick and get him sprung, then the punk start flip flopping with him. You got punks who are into turning out little young Niggas that come to the pen thinking he is so hard and know the game and thinking he can just smack up on a punk because he acts like a bitch. That's what you can't do because a lot of them punks can fight and ruthless just like us. Then we got those Niggas in here who are ass whole bandits. All they talk about is knocking out motha fuckas and running up in him, always with the sex jokes and scoping out a victim to run up in. I don't know what be going through the minds of the sick ass Niggas, minds like that, but whatever it is I know it is some real fucked up shit. I know that and then the little locs come through with the pant hanging all around they Some of the homies who know booty bandits, be plotting and hoping they mess up so he could run up in them. Cuzz the prison is wicket; it all goes down in here. The homies raping other homies who done raped a lil homie. The homie sexual assaulting homies who been bringing in the dope and not kicking down and got together to rob him and do all type of other shit to him. Then you got homies who move a lil homie into the room with him. End up getting the lil homie high and then running up in him. Normally Niggas who do shit like that, be from the same hood of their victims and other crips can't really say much of nothing about it, because that is a hood issue, not a crips issue. One thing about those united slob nations you will never hear nothing about them raping their homies or fucking punk's. Them slobs will kill a Nigga behind attempting to do something like that let alone doing it. Also, the Muslims will also, the non-pork eating motha fuckers are not to be fucked with either unless you want some serious problems. They are like them slobs they push a strict line. Cuzz, we loc's are the only ones who can't get our shit together. We would be the biggest gang on the street and in prison if we could just stop tripping with each other and stop wanting to run shit when we are not capable to lead and clean up our back yards. Us the Muslims and the lobs make up for the blacks in prison. There are other gangs, but we are the major ones, the biggest and spread nationwide.

"How do crips view the police, how they feel about them?" I asked.

Loc, all black gangs hate them especially us. It is Crip with us; the police are one of our biggest enemies. Now that this three strike law is being picked up around different states they trying to bust us for anything to strike us out, and we killing anything in the way that keep up from getting away, police, kid's old folks, dog's, it don't matter all by standers are getting peeled, If you want to stick your nose in shit that don't concern you. We are going to put some holes in you too. The polices who wants to be super cops we are letting them have the barrels of ak's, Hk's, Uzis, Teck's, Mp-5's, anything that's going to shoot a lot of bullets, because we were trying to smoke their asses. It's already been made official with street gangs that we are holding court on the street. Shoot to kill all polices when being pursued. If you going to go to prison for life you might as well go with a bang and kill as many polices as you can before they catch you. If you get away then you done well, but if you don't you still done gun, by killing a one time. This is the mentality that has been adopted on the streets. That's why we are packing heavy artillery. That's why we don't pull over for the cops. That is why we blast immediately. The stricter laws they make the more ruthless we become to avoid prison. This is how we think inside the prisons; also, why shouldn't we kill the police if thy harm one of ours. What can they do to us when most of us already have life sentences and already in prison? Why shouldn't we kill other inmates who push us to get violent with them, if we going to stab them, we might as well take their life? That's our mentality of not only the crips but all the gangs now. We can't even be mad at how we are even being treated, because we chose the life style we wanted to live, and when you choose to be part of a gang or be involve with criminal activities then you should know you are not always going to be a winner, and the bad do follow the good. A gangster just has to suck it up and deal with whatever that comes his way.

3

Southerner Mexican's

"What are Southerner Mexicans?" I asked.

We are South Sider's "Surenos". A Mexican gang who represents the south, the big el uno el trece. Trece is our number it's the 13th letter of the Alphabet, and the M that stands for Mexican. All South Siders are not Surenos, in order to become a Surenos you must first put in work. You must earn your respect to be a Surenos by putting in a lot of work for the La Raza.

"What are the differences between the South Siders and the Surenos?" I asked.

South Siders are the first stage of our gang. When you are honored to become a Surenos, you gain the respect of all, South Siders who are now beneath you. A Surenos main goal then is to reach the level of respect to be made into a big homie; Mexican Mafia and Mexican Mafia are our big homies. We are under them. We are their arms and legs we take care of all their missions and business dealings that need to be handled regardless what that mission or business is, if they say do it, we must do it. And it will be done. The only way to be made a big homie, you first have to become a Surenos, then you must put in a lot of work for the big homies a lot of killings and make sure they are receiving their 1/3 of all drug sells from all the South Sider gangs and keep order in the barrios. As a prospective we are sent on many missions, and once we complete all the missions successfully and earn the trust and respect of the big homies. Then we would be made, giving our number, the date that we were born, and Made into Mexican Mafia, we are given our own area, our own prison, our own jail. We collect 1/3 from all Southerner gang's in that area and run them how we see fit. Once a Mexican Mafia no other Southerner Mexican can harm you or refuse to do what you say, or he will be taken out. The only person could bring harm to you is another big homie, Mexican Mafia.

The big homies are the ones who stopped all the South Siders from doing drive bys and killing up our people. There are many different Southern Mexican gangs, who are South Siders that use to kill each other, but the big homies stop all that and brought the hoods together under the SUR "Soldier Under Recognition." The big homies are a collective of Mexicans who use to be south Siders. The leaders of different Southern gangs, who had the love and respect of their hoods, they seen how we was killing up own people, gang banging, and they came together and decided to bring everyone together and take over the drug industry and build up our barrios. Open up our own businesses take over the hoods in each state. Any South Sider who refused to follow their orders got the Green light. They are killed if they don't want to follow orders. Every Southern Mexican hood are taxed 1/3 every month of all the drugs they sell. This money goes to the big homies to create businesses, by land, build the hood and support those in prisons refusal to pay you get the Green Light. All South Siders and Surenos are obligated to the big homies. You must be willing to place your life on the line for them at any giving time with pride. Each and every Mexican member must be willing to sacrifice his life when honor comes available to you, and if he wishes not to do his duty he will be taking out.

"Can you tell me how the Southerners run their program in prison?" I asked.

Every yard has a key holder who is a Sureno. He is the head for all the Southern Mexican's, when any South Sider comes to the prison, we all are under one set of rules as Raza. No individual sets. All Mexican must show us their paper work. We need to know your full name, age, what hood you from, your nick name, how much time you got, what other prisons you been to, and what type of tattoos you have. All this information is written down and saved. It is his name we will check to see if he is not in good standers with the homies. We get a list of homies names every month that has the green light on them. Once his name is checked over the list and he check's out ok, and then we will provide him with everything he needs to make his time as comfortable as possible. He will be introduced to all the homies on the yard. His roommate is obligated to school him on how things are running on the yard, and if he doesn't check out in good standers, we will lift him off the yard immediately. We don't allow no rat's molesters, rapist, drive bye shooter, or Mexican Homosexuals to walk the main line. We will roll them up off the yard. We try to send this type of disgrace to our race out in a body bag. There will be no south side Mexican on the yard that is not function with the La Raza. We are not excepting no excuses. There will be no we found God and now giving your life to being Christian or any other religion, if you haven't found SUR, and then we are rolling you up, there will be no cops out. Any Mexican who shows a sign of weakness, we will lift him. Weakness is not allowed among the SUR Familia. We have mandatory rules that all Mexicans must follow. Every member must be up before the program starts. There is no sleeping while programs are up and running. You can go to sleep after the program shuts down. Your mattress must be rolled up. The cell must be kelp clean neat. Not fighting with your celly, if there is a problem let another member know so we can get one of them moved into another cell with a homie who they can get along with, everyone must study anything educational to keep the mind strong, your clothes must be neat, heads shaved. The reason why we keep our heads shaved is if one of us stabs someone and the officer happens to see it, we can blend in with the group of the homies and it would be hard to pick out the one whom they saw doing the stabbing. All the homies have to come out to the yard when they are allowed. If not then they get punish with 113 count burpies, if you sick and can't make it out to the yard for whatever reason you still will get punished with 113 count. You can either do them on the yard the next day or in the unit, but they must be done, and a homie must be there to witness you doing them. There is absolutely no prison Robberies. No disrespecting the police, because if a police officer disrespects you then you are obligated to stab him. So, to avoid any problems, is to show respect at all times, speak to them when spoken to or when you need something that they can only issue out and never start playing with them, also there are no head up fights with any blacks and if one fights, we all fight. No coming out to the yard intoxicated. We have a daily work out program it doesn't matter what you do as long as you work out for an hour and half is good. We are told that we are not allowed to use drugs because we must stay alert at all times, but if the key holder uses, he allows everyone else too use if they choose. On other yards the key holder may not use so we will not be able to. "Do the southerners rape other inmates?" I asked.

Only if they looking to be sent out of here in a body bag, we will not except any of our people raping any one and we will not allow for anyone else to rape any of ours. If a homie is even caught sex playing, he might get rolled up, but for sure he will have issue coming and have to do lean up. When a homie has to do clean up, that is when the key holder decides that it's time to clean up our back yard. That mean to lift those who are not in good standers with the Familia any more. So those who got clean up do are the ones who have to go and lift those who need to be lifted. Cleaning house, cleaning the back yard it means the same. If you got clean up duties it must be done when you are told do it. This type of duty can put a homie in bad position to getting more time if not life; because he may have attacked his victim right in front of the police and even the police if he tries to interfere it's a must that he gets his target.

"Do the Southerners sell drugs in the prison?" I asked.

Si-Yes, we push pounds of drugs through the prisons monthly, Crystal, Heroin, and weed. We sell to everyone except the Northenos, Black's, and homosexuals, the reason why we don't sell to Blacks because we are not allowed to do business with them. The Blacks never can deal straight. Plus, the big homies had put the green light on all blacks because back in the days. A Crip spit on one of the big homies in court, and ever sense then we been killing each other, especially in Los Angeles, on the streets in the jails and in prison. We have been going at it for years. Plus, those crips feel they are running things and always disrespecting, we Surenos have a real big hate for crips.

"Why is the Green light on all Blacks and not just the Crips?" I asked.

The reason is due to when a Mexican kill or harms a Crip member. The bloods jump in because they look at it as a race issue then we have to war with them over something they don't have nothing to do with. The big homie know it would happen like this because the bloods always end up backing the crips or the crips in up backing the bloods when it come fighting and to the race other than black. That why he put the light on all blacks. We really didn't have no problems with the bloods we use to do a lot of business on the streets with the UBN's, but that ended when they decided to get involve in our business and the killed up a few homies and Robbed them for a bunch of heroin and crystal.

Then the Northenos they been our arch enemies they want the same thing we want, to control the streets, drugs, prison and have the power. We got a big hate for them because all side black Mexicans are always trying to act black. They talk like blacks, dress like blacks, walk like blacks, hang with blacks, listen to black music, eat and drink after blacks. That why we call them blackxicans (Black Mexicans) they even ride with blacks on the streets and in prison. The normally hang strong with the bloods for they both gang colors are red. They need to learn how to stick with they own race.

We sell all our drugs to the woods and the others, we never have problems out of the other, but the woods they tend to slow drag about paying and some even would get a nice size

Clavo from us and can't pay, he even might P.C. up off the yard before we could get to him. So, we'll slap the dept on his people, if they refuse to pay then we go to war, that's why we now have a policy not to give no wood more than a hundred dollars' worth of dope at a time. Once they pay then we will sell them more. We make big feddy off of drugs. Drugs is how support our gang in prison. This how we keep our girls coming to visit and bringing up the clavo's. We buy transportation for certain homies girls, so they could car pull and bring the other homie girls up to visit the homeboys, any dope that the homies bring in we must give 1/3 of it to the key holder. Basically, we are paying Tax, and if we have a problem with collecting money from someone, we sold drugs to, we just let the key holder know and he will send someone to do the collecting

"How do you southerners feel about the Wood's?" I asked.

We don't care for any of them like we know they don't care for us. We been riding with each other for a long time, but we don't need their help. Woods think they are the Superior race and we know that we are the SUR, and we sometimes have issues over this. The little Nazi woods are a true hate group and we know they don't car for us at all, but we will take flight on them all. It has happened before on many of occasions. All we request from all races is respect. Give us respect we will not have no problems, disrespect us we will go to war.

14

NORTHERNER MEXICANS

"What are Northerner Mexicans?"

"Chicano's from the north side. We are the Northern Familia, Northenos 14.

"Tell Me about what the Northern Familia stands for?" I asked.

The Northern family is a gang of north side Chicanos who come together to protect our hoods, to support our communities to establish our own businesses, markets, build our own communities make a better life and way for our families so we can get out of the ghettos and own our own homes and send our folks to the colleges. We gangsters choose to put our lives on the line every day to make our vision a reality. We place ourselves in dangerous situations of being killed or sent to the pen for life in order to make money to build our dreams. Most of us are into criminal activities pushing the dope, robbery, jacking sewer rat's drug houses. Jacking cars for chop shop, you name it, we just about do it. It's all for a cause though for the establishment and strengthening of the northern Familia enterprise and communities, we are paving the way for our lil brothers, sisters, cousins to be able to have opportunities that wasn't available to us. We have now done well so far with or vision and goals. We got many businesses of our own and provide jobs to the homies, car clubs who support fundraiser, record labels, markets, car washes, and many of my folks going back to school and colleges even some of the homies is stepping back into the school's and trade schools.

"What about the prison, why so many of you going to prison?" I asked.

"Like I said before and I'll tell you again we involve ourselves in criminal activities to make that money or have to put an enemy to rest who threatens the Familia. A lot of us are so caught up into the gangster life style that we refuse to change our ways. We rather are involved in doing the dirty work and allowing the younger generation to live out our dreams for us. I know that sounds crazy but its real. Some of us can't read or write and have been in the street life all our lives and involved in so much shit trying to make end meat for us to go back to school would be a waste of our time and the teachers time are minds have already been programmed for one thing to survive by the means of the streets. So gangstas like us is pushing the young homies into staying in school to be better than us not just like us. When you are doing dirt, you bound to get caught up and we all know the punishment for that, jail, prison, or the grave yard. But when you are in the life style of being a gangsta you don't think about those consequences.

"How do the Northerners run their program inside the prison?" I asked.

"We run a smooth program with strict rules but still a smooth program. A new homie that comes through we get at him and holler at him to get a feel to whom he is and where he is from. We run down the rules, find out if he needs anything and if so, all the homies would pitch in a nice care package, and one of the homies who has an extra radio, or tube they would shoot it his way to use. We keep the north family clean of the molesters, and rappers. The homies do everything together. We all keep a close eye on each other. Our numbers don't always be big in other prison and those sewer rats like to trip when they see us out numbered. That's just how they are; they won't box because they know me have major scraps. The only thing they would try to do is rat pack you three and up on one person. So, we have to stay ready and keep big knives just in case they run up. We hang out with the Blacks, we use the same phones, showers, workout area, eat at the same tables with them. We feel more comfortable around blacks; most of us grew up with black, and have black friends, so it's a love thing. The sewer rats feel that we try to be like the blacks. They say we are a disgrace to the Mexican race. They call us Blackicans. We don't trip; we just handle our business every time they feel like they want a problem. When the homies are short in numbers the Damus always catch our back. We are a lot closer to the Damus then any other blacks or black gangs. They always have been straight with us from the beginning. Those Crips is the one's we leery of. Just put it this way, they can't be trusted and that's real, too scandalous. We try to keep all dealings with them at a minimum. They really don't like us that much because we kick it with the Damus though. The united Blood Nation, Blood line, and pirus they are some real cool people and if a Damu tells you something you can basically depend on it. Most of them are loyal to their word, plus they are not disrespectful."

"The wood's, we only put up with them because that's one of the biggest money sources for the drugs you make a lot of money off the mint leaf, trees with the blacks, but the heroin and crank, that's the woods drugs and they would give up everything in their cell for a fat paper. The others money is also good as well, but they don't buy as much as the Wood's do, plus when the sewer rats are not in pocket, they use the others to come and buy the drugs from us. We bring in our own dope or work with a Damu to help us get it in if they got the hook up. We usually help each other. The money that we make from selling drugs in the prison, we break bread with our ladies for personal use, to recoup, and expenses. To put money to live inside the prison especially if you want homo stabbed. There are other races who do fuck around with punks but that's they business our business is Northern Familia, fourteens business."

"How do Northerners feel about the police?" I asked.

"We don't like any police because we are on two different sides. We do blast on the police on the streets and in prison. We are not into making friends with them, but we do try to get up under a female officer so she could bring in the drugs. Even the men officers they are just as easy to get especial those new one's who just started working. Everyone likes money and don't mine a little extra. We have been having our home boys and home girls who haven't been into any trouble to apply for correctional jobs. So, we could have some inside assistance to look out for us."

"Do the northerners use drugs?" I asked.

"Yeah, we do some of us. Some of use like that tree some like the other stuff. We do are thing. We even make wine and the homies will kick it, drink and smoke. Like I said we run a smooth program, we just demand that our comrades just follow the mandatory rules of the Familia and stay in shape and ready for war at all times, and to never lose sight to where they are and everything else is all good. We never have to worry about materials for knives as long as we got plastic around and mop buckets, we can make knives. There is a lot to deal with in the pen, to many crazy people with no sense, too much time on our hands with nothing to do. Too much stress and the only way of releasing it are with violent sense that's the easiest and first thought that comes to mind. You can always find someone who is willing to challenge you. Fist fighting is out, a knife playing is in. This is the prison way for all races. Every race, gang, and individual in prison is dangerous, because you never know how a person is thinking from one day to the next. So, no one in the pen can be taken lightly regardless how big your crew is, how though and feared you are, no matter how many stabbings or killing you done, none of that means nothing to a man whose out to get you. You must play it smart and overlook some things that can be over looked and keep emotions and you mind together if you want to make it through the pen. Most of every one in here has this mask on hiding their true self and when a person keeps that mask long enough, he becomes that very mask, and honestly speaking many times at night when I lay in my bunk thinking, I wish that I had never ever got involve in the criminal life style and went to school and didn't hang out with the homies smoking and drinking and doing crime and everything else we did. If it wasn't for me wanting to be cool, and hang out, and get a respiration that I have now, which don't mean nothing to no one but me and my homies. I wouldn't be locked up with all this time I have to do. I wouldn't be going through mental trips with my selves at night, I would be in so much emotional pain, having to watch my back every day all day, I wouldn't have to eat soups and chips and peanut butter sandwiches when I get hungry or smell another man's shit or listen to him piss every day, I would have to worry about who's my girl out their giving up the panties to and if she wrote me, I wouldn't have to wash my clothes out of buckets, the sink, or the toilet. I wouldn't have to worry about if today is going to be my last day on this earth, I wouldn't even be thinking about all the people in my family I hadn't told I love them. Only if I want a dumb ass and chosen this bull shit life style. I would be at home right now thinking of no of this, living life on the streets. Even if I was poor and had nothing, no friends, no money, girl, place to stay, family, and no identity, I would except that grateful, then be locked up and if there was a way that I could give my old life back just for my freedom. I would give it all back, the keys to the gang, my rep, my name, my homies, the money, low riders, everything and I hate to say it even my race I would give it all back to live that square life. But since that's not possible, I might as well keep being that gangsta that I am to the fullest and keep my personal thoughts to my selves. I am sure everyone on this prison has thought one time or another hat they would have made a different choice. They may never admit it, but the prison its self is the toughest, hardest and coldest gangsta that it is who can never be killed unless you never enter its gates, that the real key holder.

Author Notes

My Analysis about the prison, the different prison gang's and their functions that comes from actual experience and living within the realms of the wall's most of the inmates don't care to much about any education. As long as the drugs, cigarettes, televisions and other entertainment appliances are available they are content with that. Majority of the inmates have life sentences that have given up and accepted the prison life style and won't allow their minds to venture beyond these walls. There is a hand full that stays diligently working at regaining their freedom, by studying the Law Day in and day out. You have those who study and read books all day and educate them self's through the means of available books. The Muslims are one of the strongest forces, if not the strongest in all aspects. They believe in educating the mind and keeping the body strong. They eliminate themselves from the prison politics, and they're not into dealing drugs, or in the use of them. Nothing that would intoxicate the mind and body is permitted for use amongst them. What I also noticed about the Muslims is they tend to have a problem with the Nation of Islam Muslims. The Nation of Islam, Muslims normally would have their own community. They believe in discipline, structure, educating themselves from the cradle to the grave and teaching their people history which is Black history, and trying to bring others in to Islam. The problem that the two groups of Muslims have is because of the different beliefs concerning the Muslim religion, but one thing I noticed that they still remain together as one solid mass as Muslim.

The Christian inmates don't involve themselves into nothing that has to do with violence or the prison politics within the Christian group there are a mixture of races. These are the inmates who go to church and proclaim that they are Christian and not involve with the prison activities or gangs. That means nothing to any of the prison gangs especially the Southern Mexicans, if you are a Southern Mexican you will follow under their rules regardless if you Christian or not are, they will lift you off the yard, also when a race riot occurs, being a Christian doesn't stop any other race from stabbing them. The gangs don't care about any of that, if their race is at war with another race and they are in reach, they will get a knife ran in them without a second thought.

There are many different gangs inside the prisons. The Blacks has the most separation amongst themselves than any other race of people, but they will all quickly come together when their race is threatened by another race. They are also quick to stab each other. The Wood's which they call them self's the Wood Pile they are a vicious dare devil type of gang. They are very dangerous and suicidal. They have no problem risking it all. They create the most wicked type of prison made knifes ever seen and will attack a person in from of an officer if they have planned to get you. They are also known for stabling officers as well and having no problem with doing so. They don't care about the consequences or repercussions, as long as they take care of their main objection all else is fair. They are very strange in their way of behavior, and don't see anything wrong with hugging and kissing each other, sex playing and talking about having sex with another man. Most are drug addicts who love to shoot dope, speed and heroin. Those are the highs of choice. A lot of them love that speed. When they get on that drug, they seem to become more creative, sexually active, hideous, and super hyper. It's no telling what they might do once they get to tweaking off that dope, but regardless of all the drug's they may indulge in they still are a dangerous group of people and shouldn't be under estimated, because they are the ones who normally have all the steel and biggest best made knifes you ever seen, and will put them to use immediately. They are also the ones who make prison bombs have the liquid poisons that they put in food and drinks which is undetectable by taste, smell or seen by the naked eye. One thing about the woods they will do business with all races as long as they have the drugs they will spend or trade for items.

The Nazi skin heads are a totally different bread of white boys. The Woods really don't like them, but they allow them to stay on the lines because they are the same race and it keeps the white race stronger. The skin heads hate all races. They keep their heads shaved bold, only do business among them self's. They are a wild bunch, very hyper with each other and strict when it comes to dealing with other races. Most of them either have the Nazi Germany Swastika, lightning bolts, or the number 88 tattooed on their body. They are always eager to prove them self, wants to be recognized by others as a tough and vicious gang. They often make examples out of their own race by preying on the weak white boys who come into the prison system, who no involve in any gang activities. They start by trying to recruit him; it normally ends up that their potential recruitment will be reluctant and inclined to be subjected to such beliefs and politics. So, the skins will begin their exhorting tactics and when the money runs dry, they will end up gang raping him and threaten his life. They target the younger white boys, who has no ties with any Wood's, and they carry out their tactics. If there is any type of resistance shown towards them, they will all take flight and try to kill that person. The skin heads always have problems with the Woods, and they tend to fight and stab each other over disagreements. After their little exhibition is over, everything goes right back to normal and there's no grudges between the two. They look at the battle as a training program to keep them ready for the real enemies. This away of thinking is also weird to me.

The Southerner Mexicans are united as one gang. There's no distinction with them and the only internal problems they have is when one of them disobey or break a rule or there a snitch coming into the prison that they have to deal with the blacks believe that the Southerners are racist, but most Southerners are not. They are forced to follow suit with the politics and rules that have been laid down for them or risk loosening their life for going against the grain. They have a real strict policy and when a rule is broken there's no slap on the hand there will be a punishment of some sort, knowing that there is no room for laws, they just follow all the rules and do what they have to do and told to do by the southerner who has the authority for that prison. They move around the yard in packs and do everything together. They have a relationship with the whites and from my observation the Southerners have installed a little fear into the Wood's. I also notice that the skin heads will not listen to the Southerner's and will take flight (attack) them. The also love to shoot heroin and smoke speed, but they have a policy, that no southerner will come out to the yard high for any reason. They get high in their cells and remain there until the high is gone down. The Southerners are also very sneaky; they are always plotting to do some under handed sneak attacks of some sort. They also don't allow any Mexican homosexuals to walk the mainline with them. If one comes to the yard, they immediately send a hitter to lift him up off the yard, they see homosexuals as disrespect to their race. The Southerners are very respectful to all races that are something they take pride in. The southerners don't only fight with the Blacks, whites, and Northern Mexicans, but also the others. The others are a classified individual who ethnicity is different then, Black, white, or Mexican. They are individuals who are from different countries overseas, and Islands. They stick together on the prison yards. They don't call them self's a gang and don't have a political structure, they are more of a neutral group who deals and do business with all races and try not to get involved with the gang activity on the yards the officers favor the others because they never get into any problems. So, they are providing with over 90% of the critical jobs in prison the program clerk positions, cooks, food servers, yard crew, building porters. Normally when the prison goes on lock down the others would only be the ones not on lock down after a twenty-four-hour emergency assessment period is completed, and then all the other's critical workers are released to normal program while all the other races remain on lock down.

The Crips have it the hardest inside the prisons because there are so many different Crip gangs on the yards. So, when one gets into something on the yard the institution will lock down all Crip gang members. I also notice that the crips make their own rules as they feel amongst them, and they are not all together as a whole. Every group wants to be the chief, and don't want to follow up under one voice, regardless if that voice could lead them to success. The crips seems to have an egotistical problem. Every fraction wants to be identified as notorious, tough, and crazy, which they really are mentally challenged. They want the fame and top respect of all gangs, so they normally try to outdo each other when it comes to three moments of violent acts. Plus, they are not trust worthy their works is no good, they care not what you feel about them as long as you recognize they will kill and stomp your face into the ground without any remorse. They are conniving, selfish, disrespectful, could hearted, and out of control with my optic point of view. Dealing with a Crip is like striking your hand into a blazing dire when you knowing you're going to get burn. All Crip gang members are not just Black you have white boy's, Mexicans and different other races who are Crips, when they come into the prisons the administration will classify them as Black regardless of their original ethnicity and Black regardless of their original ethnicity and house them with a Black Crip gang member. A lot of it and will go to war with the crips over it. They will make every attempt to try and kill the Crip that's of their race. Issues like that forces all the other Blacks to get involve, because the Blacks looks at it like an attack on their race and they will not have any other race trying to harm their people. The Crips has some wicked ways, and, in these prisons, they will gang rape one of their own for being a coward and weak. Some are just into having sex with other men and looks for a reason to rape someone. The young Crips who comes to the prison for the first time seem to become the victims of rape or they come in fearing the unknown that they are willing to give sexual favors to a Crip who they feel could protect them. In the prisons rape is very seldom reported to the officers do to fear of being killed, humiliation, teased, or just in a state of denial of the fact that they had been raped. Prison rapes does occur quite often, a lot more then it is made known and spoken about and crips are not the only gangs who carry out such tactic's as these there are a lot of sick, disgusting, deranged minded people behind these walls. You would never be able to tell just by their appearance and daily actions.

The Northerner Mexican's are laid back and seem not to be always up tight or stressed out over anything. They keep a cheerful personality. They are not the type of gang that looks for problems, or prey on the weak. They don't involve them self's into homosexual activities, and not into raping their people. They have a hip style; speak street slang and a similar liking of style and taste as the blacks.

The Blood's is well respected even by their worst enemies, which are the Crips. The Bloods are a solid structure and well organized. They carry them self's in a respectful manner and is not boastful in their actions and achievement's.

Blood's seemed to be out number when it comes to the crips by 5 to 1 if not more. The Bloods are mentally stronger, well organized and rational mentally stronger, well organized and rational thinkers. They are not quick to place their whole car into a wreck, unless danger presents itself and they must react to protect them self's. I have noticed the Bloods will not rat pack another Blood member if he has an internal problem with another member. He is afforded the opportunity to a head up fight. The Bloods do not tolerate a snitch in their family. They are a vicious gang, just by looking at them or inter acting around them they don't seem to be as vicious and violent as they are. If there's a problem with one blood you will have a problem with them all and believe me, they are going to strictly come to take care of business. They don't care how big a gang or group is, if they have a problem with a group. A hand full of Blood's would rush the entire group and stab as many people as possible in that crowd. They don't believe in raping, and they will lift you from the yard if you are caught messing around with a homosexual and will kill you if you rape a blood. The Bloods are even respected by the prison gangs except for the Crips.

Those who were not involved into the street life that comes to prison, they try to stay in the shadow of the prison. They manly keep to them self's and try their best not to be noticed and tend to restrain their selves to the confinement of their cell's. They don't look to meet new friends and have very limited conversation, if any with others. It is the mechanism of staying safe and avoiding life treating situations from the on-going prison violent.

The meals in prison are just enough to keep you from starving and having extreme hunger pains. The prison taught remedy to avoid the hunger pains is to drink a 16oz glass of water before the meal and right after. This method would give you the sensation of feeling full. That's why it's very important to have store in your cell, that's if you have the financial means to purchase some. Being caught on lock down without any canteen, you will feel every moment of that lock down and most likely will lose a lot of weight.

Prison is not a place to ask other inmates to borrow or let you have anything because a price of some sort comes along with that borrowed items or giving one. The best policy is not to ask or except anything from any one if you have any artistic skills like drawing then, drawing a few different types of cards can be a way to get the needed items.

Inside the prisons there are a lot of dirty, crooked and vindictive officers. I am speaking from personal knowledge and actual dealings with several crooked officers. I have also seen a lot of things that they do. What everyone must understand is that officers are human beings also, who has emotions, who lies and steals and who are egotistic, and have different options. Although they are correctional officers that doesn't make them honest or trust worthy or even loyal to their job description, there are correctional officers who bring the drugs into the prison to make the extra money that the inmate gives them for smuggling in the drugs for him. There are also officers who gamble with inmates for money on sports, there are officers who pay inmates for money on sports, there are officers who pay inmates to beat down certain inmates that they don't like, and they give up who are snitching.

This is what I learned, seen, viewed and experienced inside the prisons and this is how it is behind the prison walls.

GLOSSARY

Bee: word use by blood gang member in a sentence that means see

Bicking: Kicking back, relaxing, resting, parlaying.

Bigarette: Cigarette

Black: Literally means completely dark; color, of or referring to back folks, here it means and referred to as heroin.

Blackxican: A word to describe a Mexican who acts like black folk, which has the black race ways.

Black Girl: Originally means female of the black race. Here it means heroin

Blast: Means to stab someone with a knife.

Blood: it is a term used by blood gang members and associates. It expresses familiarity. It informs other gang members of their allegiance. It is used informally by blood gang members to greet other Blood gang members to greet other

Blood gang members or a non-gang member. It is also used to disrespect adversary gang members.

Bone Crusher: A prison made knife made of strength

Booty Bandit: A prisoner who indulges in homosexual activities, who allures, lurks for new potential victims to have anal sex with.

Burpies: A aerobic exercise, standing, squat, go into a push up position do a push up then with draw your legs back up under you and stand back up. It's down in one continuous motion.

Brazy: Means crazy deranged, foolish, insane.

Cap: A Chap Stick cap amount of marijuana.

Christmas tree: A name referred to marijuana

Clavo: A large amount of a substance usually drugs.

Cleaning house; here it means an extreme disrespect to the crips.

Crab: Here it means an extreme disrespect to the crips.

Crank: a name referred to methamphetamine.

Crip: adversary gang of the Bloods. The word is expressed to inform other Crip gang members of their allegiance it is used by Crip gang members of their allegiance.

It is used by Crip gang members to acknowledge other members of Crip gangs.

Cuzz: A word that is freely used by Crip gang members and associates it is used to greet fellow members and nonmembers and to disrespect their adversaries.

Damu: Means Blood in Swahili language.

Drank: A wine referred to as, alcohol, Pruno, white lightn.

Glass: a name referred to methamphetamine

Go fast: a name referred to methamphetamine

Greenary: a name referred to as marijuana

Green light: a hit that is ordered on a person's life or a gang to be killed immediately or when the opportunity presents its self.

Heat: a name referred to a knife, or shank.

Head: blow job, sucking a penis.

Lift: here it means to get the person off the yard by stabbing

Kitty: contributions giving to a designated party for the assistance of the needy.

Loc: a word referred to a Crip gang member

Mint leaf: name referring to marijuana

Nip: a word uses to disrespect and degrade the Asian race.

Others: foreigners of another country island and places.

Powder: name referring to cocaine

Pruno: name referred to wine.

Reach around: a person who is giving anal sex and at the same time reach in front of his partner to jack him off (masturbation of another person at the same time having anal sex with him).

Smoke: Referred to marijuana

Snow: referred to cocaine

South Sider: Southerner Mexican

Speed: referred to methamphetamine

Tar: referred to heroin

Tree: referred to marijuana

Tweed: Referred to marijuana

White lightn: Alcohol

White Sinister: Methamphetamine

Wood: White boy

Black Panther Press
www.bpppress.com
REVOLUTION
Mandowfutur.com
Fashion

HUNTINGTON
BEACH CALIFORNIA:
KANE KUT
MURDER TRIAL
Demon with A Camera
GWENDOLYN KENNEDY
HUNTINGTON BEACH CALIFORNIA: KANE KUT MURDER TRIAL